Contents

Book Cover by [Artist]

Illustrations by [Illustrator]

[Edition Number] edition [Year of Publication]

Introduction

"Traveling – it leaves you speechless, then turns you into a storyteller." – Ibn Battuta

Welcome to the land of endless discovery, where ancient traditions harmonize with cutting-edge innovation, and every corner holds a story waiting to be unraveled. As you embark on the pages of this travel guide, allow me to guide you through the enchanting tapestry of Japan's culture, history, and natural beauty.

My name is V. Dharani Sudarvannan, I am just like you—a traveler filled with curiosity and a desire to explore the world. While I may not be a seasoned globe-trotter, my journey through Japan has been one of awe, wonder, and countless discoveries. I hope to share this sense of wonder and excitement with you through this guide, as we navigate Japan's diverse landscapes and vibrant culture together.

In the following pages, you will find a comprehensive resource designed to provide you with the knowledge and tools needed to navigate Japan easily and confidently, even if it's your first time traveling abroad. Whether you're planning a short getaway or a long-term adventure, this guide is here to help you make the most of your time in Japan. From practical tips on transportation and accommodation to in-depth explorations of Japan's cultural highlights, each chapter is meticulously crafted to provide the information you need to make the most of your time in Japan.

But this guide is more than just a compilation of facts and figures; it is a companion that seeks to inspire and empower you to embark on a journey of discovery. Alongside detailed descriptions of must-visit attractions and insider recommendations, you will find anecdotes and insights that offer a glimpse into the soul of Japan – its traditions, customs, and way of life. Whether you're a history buff eager to explore ancient temples and samurai castles or a foodie on the hunt for the perfect bowl of ramen, there is something here for everyone.

So, whether you're dreaming of strolling through the cherry blossom-lined streets of Kyoto, soaking in the vibrant energy of Tokyo's bustling neighborhoods, or hiking through the misty mountains of rural Japan, let this guide be your compass as you embark on your Japanese adventure. With each turn of the page, you'll discover new wonders, forge unforgettable memories, and come one step closer to unraveling the magic of Japan.

So, without further ado, let us begin our journey as we unlock the mysteries and magic of Japan together, starting with the vibrant streets of Tokyo. As we delve deeper into the heart and soul of this captivating country, may you find inspiration, wonder, and countless moments of joy along the way.

Chapter 1

Beyond Japan: Preparing for Your Journey

To begin your incredible adventure, the first and foremost tip is all about discovering essential insights and practical advice to effectively plan your trip to Japan. From understanding cultural norms to budgeting, this chapter equips you with useful tools for a smooth and memorable travel experience in Japan. Additionally, we'll explore practical tips for budgeting and financial planning, ensuring that you make the most of your resources while enjoying all that Japan has to offer. Whether you're a first-time traveler or a seasoned explorer, this chapter will equip you with the knowledge and tools to prepare effectively and embark on a seamless journey through the Land of the Rising Sun.

1.1 Booking Your Flights

Booking Your Flights

→ Tips for Finding Affordable Flights:

To secure the best deals on flights to Japan, utilize fare comparison websites such as Skyscanner, Google Flights, and Kayak. These platforms offer extensive databases, allowing you to compare prices from numerous airlines and travel agencies. With intuitive interfaces and flexible search options, they simplify finding affordable flights. Features like price tracking, flexible date searches, and price alerts empower you to pinpoint the most cost-effective options.

→ Flexibility with Travel Dates and Departure Airports:

Adjust your travel dates to off-peak times or mid-week, as this can often result in lower fares. Similarly, exploring flights from different departure airports allows you to compare prices and find potential savings. Sometimes, flying from an alternative airport can offer more budget-friendly options.

→ Booking in Advance:

Booking your flights to Japan in advance can be advantageous for securing lower prices, particularly for popular travel periods. Research indicates that the optimal time to book international flights is typically two to three months before departure. Monitoring fares and booking early when favorable deals arise can help you maximize savings.

→ Additional Costs:

Beyond the base fare, consider the total cost of your flight, including additional charges such as baggage fees, seat selection charges, and onboard meal costs. When choosing between budget airlines and full-service carriers, weigh the potential savings against the supplementary costs associated with budget carriers, such as stricter baggage policies and added fees.

→ Special Promotions and Discounts:

Keep an eye out for special promotions and discounts that airlines may offer. Monitoring airline promotions and sales and subscribing to airline newsletters or following them on social media can provide us with timely notifications about discounted fares. Seizing limited-time offers, flash sales, and promo codes promptly is crucial, as these deals often come with restricted booking windows.

1.2 Ideal Time to Visit

The ideal time to visit Japan depends on personal preferences and interests, as each season offers unique experiences. It depends on individual preferences for climate, activities, and cultural events. Let's take a closer look at each season and what it offers for travelers exploring Japan.

Spring: A Blossoming Wonderland (March-May)

As the winter chill dissipates, Japan bursts into life with the arrival of spring. March marks the beginning of cherry blossom season, or hanami, the time when the country is blanketed in delicate pink and white blooms. The peak of cherry blossom viewing typically occurs in early April, attracting visitors from all around the world to witness this iconic spectacle. Beyond the cherry blossoms, spring offers mild temperatures, making it ideal for exploring Japan's outdoor attractions. From the historic streets of Kyoto to the scenic beauty of rural areas, spring provides the perfect backdrop for sightseeing, hiking, and enjoying outdoor festivals.

Spring: A Blossoming Wonderland (March-May)

Summer: Festivals and Fireworks (June - August)

Summer in Japan brings warmer temperatures and a vibrant atmosphere filled with festivals and fireworks. From June to August, cities and towns across the country come alive with celebrations such as Tanabata, Gion Matsuri, and Obon. These festivals showcase Japan's rich cultural heritage through traditional music, dance, and food, providing visitors with a unique opportunity to immerse themselves in local traditions. While summer can be hot and humid, especially in urban areas, it's also the perfect time to enjoy outdoor activities like hiking, beach trips, and camping. Whether you're exploring the bustling streets of Tokyo or relaxing on the shores of Okinawa, summer offers a wealth of experiences for travelers to enjoy.

Summer: Festivals and Fireworks (June - August)

Autumn: A Symphony of Colors (September-November)

As the summer heat fades away, Japan transforms into a kaleidoscope of colors with the arrival of autumn. From September to November, the landscape is painted with vibrant foliage, known as koyo, ranging from fiery reds to golden yellows. This stunning natural display attracts visitors from near and far, making autumn one of the most popular times to visit Japan. With cooler temperatures and fewer crowds, it's an excellent time for sightseeing and outdoor adventures. Whether you're exploring ancient temples in Kyoto, hiking through the scenic landscapes of Nikko, or cruising along the picturesque Lake Kawaguchi, autumn offers a serene and picturesque backdrop for your travels.

Autumn: A Symphony of Colors (September-November)

Winter: Snowy Escapes and Cozy Retreats (December - February)

As temperatures drop and snow blankets the landscape, Japan takes on a magical charm in winter. From December to February, northern regions like Hokkaido transform into winter wonderlands, offering opportunities for skiing, snowboarding, and snowshoeing.

Winter: Snowy Escapes and Cozy Retreats (December - February)

Iconic snow festivals such as the Sapporo Snow Festival attract visitors with elaborate ice sculptures and illuminated displays. While temperatures can be cold, especially in the north, winter also provides the perfect excuse to indulge in Japan's hot springs, onsen, and warm comfort foods like hot pots and steaming bowls of ramen. Whether you're soaking in a rotenburo (outdoor hot spring) surrounded by snow-capped mountains or savoring seasonal delicacies by the fireplace, winter in Japan offers a cozy and enchanting retreat from the outside world.

1.3 Budget Planning

In the Budget Planning subsection, we'll dive into actionable advice for effectively managing your finances during your trip to Japan. When we discuss budgeting for a trip, it's essential to consider all potential costs, including accommodations, transportation, meals, and activities. Research average daily expenses in Japan and allocate your budget accordingly, make sure to set aside extra funds for unexpected expenses. For example, the average daily cost for a budget traveler in Japan ranges from $100 to $150, covering accommodation, meals, local transportation, and sightseeing. Bear in mind that costs may vary depending on your travel style and preferences, so adjust your budget accordingly to ensure a comfortable and enjoyable experience without overspending. To save money while traveling, consider opting for budget accommodations, using public transportation instead of taxis, and eating at local eateries rather than touristy restaurants. With careful planning and smart budgeting, you can enjoy a memorable trip to Japan without breaking the bank.

1.4 Health and Safety

Accessing the healthcare system and safeguarding belongings in Japan is relatively straightforward for travelers. Here are some tips to ensure you can get the care and minimize the risk of theft or loss.

- **Research Healthcare Options:** Before your trip, familiarize yourself with the healthcare system in Japan. Identify hospitals, clinics, and pharmacies in the areas you plan to visit. Websites and travel guides can provide valuable information.

- **Carry Important Documents:** Keep essential documents, such as your passport, travel insurance information, and any medical records or prescriptions, in a secure location. Having these documents readily available can expedite the process if you need medical assistance.

- **Travel Insurance:** Consider purchasing travel insurance that includes coverage for medical emergencies. Review your policy to understand what is covered, including medical expenses, hospitalization, and emergency medical evacuation.

- **Emergency Numbers:** Save emergency contact numbers in your phone, including local ambulance services **(119)** and the contact information for your country's embassy or consulate in Japan.

- **Language Assistance:** While many healthcare professionals in Japan speak English, communication barriers may still arise. Consider downloading translation apps or carrying a phrasebook to facilitate communication with medical staff.

- **Seek Assistance:** If you require medical attention, don't hesitate to ask for help. Hotel staff, tour guides, or locals can assist you in finding a nearby medical facility or contacting emergency services.

- **Use Anti-Theft Accessories:** Invest in anti-theft accessories such as slash-proof bags, RFID-blocking wallets, and secure luggage locks to deter thieves.

- **Be Cautious with Public Wi-Fi:** Exercise caution when using public Wi-Fi networks, especially when accessing sensitive information such as online banking or personal accounts. Use virtual private networks (VPNs) for added security.

1.5 Cultural Etiquette

In the Cultural Etiquette subsection, we delve into the significance of bowing and greetings in Japanese culture, providing travelers with essential tips to navigate social interactions respectfully. Understanding the importance of bowing, we explain its role as a gesture of respect and humility in Japanese society, emphasizing its prevalence in various contexts, from formal meetings to casual encounters. We offer practical advice on the proper execution of bows, including the appropriate angle and duration based on the level of formality and social hierarchy. Additionally, we explore the significance of greetings, such as "Konnichiwa" (hello) and "Arigatou gozaimasu" (thank you), and provide guidance on when and how to use them appropriately. To prepare for their trip, readers are encouraged to familiarize themselves with common phrases and expressions, as well as basic Japanese etiquette through language learning resources and cultural guides. By embracing these cultural norms with sincerity and respect, travelers can forge meaningful connections and enrich their experiences in Japan.

Chapter 2

Before You Depart: Essential Pre-Travel Checklist

Moving forward, our second tip emphasizes the importance of a thorough pre-travel checklist of essential tasks and preparations to complete to guarantee a hassle-free journey to Japan. From organizing travel documents to securing accommodations and packing essentials, you will learn how to ensure a smooth and stress-free travel experience.

2.1 Travel Documents

→ Visas:

Research the specific visa requirements for your nationality and purpose of travel to Japan well in advance of your trip. Visit the official website of the Embassy of Japan in your country or contact your nearest Japanese consulate for up-to-date information on visa types, application procedures, and processing times. Ensure that you submit all required documents accurately and meet any eligibility criteria to avoid delays or rejections

→ Passports:

Check the expiration date of your passport and ensure that it remains valid for at least six months beyond your intended stay in Japan. Renew your passport if necessary well in advance of your trip to avoid any issues at immigration checkpoints. Make copies of your passport's identification page and store them separately from your original passport for backup in case of loss or theft.

→ Travel Insurance:

Invest in comprehensive travel insurance that provides coverage for medical emergencies, trip cancellations, lost or stolen belongings, and other unforeseen circumstances. Compare policies from different insurance providers to find the one that offers the best coverage for your needs and budget. Carry a copy of your travel insurance policy and emergency contact information with you all the time during your trip.

→ Health Certificates:

Check if you need to provide proof of COVID-19 vaccination or negative test results for entry into Japan. Schedule any required vaccinations or tests well in advance of your departure date and ensure that you have the necessary documentation to present to immigration officials upon arrival. Stay informed about the latest health and safety guidelines issued by relevant authorities and follow recommended precautions to protect yourself and others during your trip.

→ Embassy Information:

Locate the contact details and address of your home country's embassy or consulate in Japan before your trip. Register with the embassy or consulate upon arrival to receive important updates, alerts, and assistance services during your stay. Familiarize yourself with the embassy's role in providing consular assistance, such as issuing emergency travel documents, assisting with medical emergencies, and offering legal support if needed.

By following these actionable tips, you can ensure that your travel documents are in order and that you're well-prepared for a smooth and enjoyable trip to Japan.

Essential Pre-Travel Checklist

2.2 Accommodation Reservation

When specifying your accommodation preferences for your stay in Japan, it's essential to provide clear and detailed information to ensure that all your needs are met. Here is an email template by which you can effectively communicate your requirements.

Subject: Accommodation Reservation Request

Dear [Hotel/Hostel Name],

I hope this email finds you well. My name is [Your Name], and I am planning a trip to Japan with my [family/friends/partner] in [Month, Year]. We are excited to explore the vibrant culture and rich history of Japan, and also we are currently in the process of arranging our accommodations.

We are interested in staying at your establishment during our visit to [City/Area]. Below are the details of our reservation request:

- Check-in Date: [Preferred Check-in Date]

- Check-out Date: [Preferred Check-out Date]
- Number of Guests: [Number of Adults/Children]
- Room Type: [Single/Double/Twin/Triple, etc.]
- Budget Constraints: We are looking for accommodation options within the range of [Budget Range] per night.
- Preferred Location or Neighborhood: We would prefer to stay in a central location with easy access to public transportation and nearby attractions.
- Special Requirements or Amenities: [List any specific requirements or amenities needed for a comfortable stay, such as Wi-Fi, breakfast included, non-smoking room, etc.]

We would appreciate it if you could provide us with information on room availability, rates, and any special offers or discounts available during our stay. Additionally, if possible, please include details on any additional fees or taxes that may apply to our reservation.

Please let us know if you require any further information or documentation from us to proceed with the reservation process. We are flexible with our travel dates and are open to alternative accommodation options if our preferred dates are not available.

Thank you for your attention to this matter. We look forward to hearing back from you soon, also we are eager to experience the hospitality of your establishment during our stay in Japan.

Best regards,
[Your Name]

Feel free to customize the email template with your specific travel details and preferences before sending it to your chosen accommodation provider in Japan.

By providing clear and detailed information, you can effectively communicate your accommodation needs and increase the likelihood of finding the perfect place to stay during your trip to Japan.

2.3 Transportation Arrangements

For a comprehensive transportation itinerary for a two-week trip to Japan, consider the following:

→ Researching Train Schedules:

Start your transportation arrangements by researching train schedules using online resources like HyperDia or official railway websites. Look for the best routes and departure times for your intercity travel to ensure a smooth journey.

→ Navigating Subway Routes:

For exploring major cities like Tokyo, Osaka, and Kyoto, familiarize yourself with subway maps and identify key lines and stations connecting to your destinations. This will help you navigate the subway system efficiently during your stay.

→ Booking Bus Tickets:

Consider bus options for shorter journeys or remote areas. Check schedules in advance and book tickets early to secure your seats and avoid last-minute hassles. This is particularly important for popular routes or during peak travel seasons.

→ Choosing Transportation Passes:

Compare the cost-effectiveness of transportation passes such as the Japan Rail Pass (JR Pass) or regional cards like Suica or Pasmo. Evaluate each option based on your itinerary and travel needs to determine the most economical choice.

→ Understanding Pass Prices:

Be aware of approximate prices for transportation passes. For example, JR Passes start from around ¥29,110 for a 7-day pass, on the other hand, regional cards typically require an initial deposit plus prepaid value.

→ Crafting an Efficient Itinerary:

Prioritize efficiency in navigating between destinations while considering accessibility and cost. Plan your itinerary carefully to optimize your travel experience in Japan within your budget constraints.

By crafting a detailed transportation itinerary that considers train schedules, subway routes, bus options, and transportation passes, you can efficiently navigate between destinations during your two-week trip to Japan while optimizing accessibility, cost-effectiveness, and travel efficiency.

2.4 Travel Insurance

Ensure a worry-free journey to Japan by securing comprehensive travel insurance tailored for your two-week trip. Look for policies that offer coverage for medical emergencies, trip cancellations, lost luggage, and unforeseen circumstances to safeguard your travel experience. Prioritize medical coverage, including hospitalization, doctor's visits, medications, and emergency evacuation. Additionally, ensure that your insurance reimburses non-refundable expenses such as flights, accommodations, and tour bookings in case of unforeseen events like illness, injury, or natural disasters. Mitigate the risk of lost or delayed luggage by selecting a policy with baggage loss or theft coverage. Review the policy's terms carefully to understand coverage limits, deductibles, and exclusions, especially for pre-existing conditions or high-risk activities. Keep emergency contact numbers and policy information readily accessible for quick travel assistance. With comprehensive travel insurance, you can confidently explore Japan, knowing you're prepared for unforeseen events.

2.5 Health Precautions

→ Vaccinations:

Ensure you have up-to-date information on routine vaccinations and consider additional vaccines for Japan, such as hepatitis A and B, Japanese encephalitis, and typhoid, based on your travel plans and personal health history.

→ Food and Water Safety:

Exercise caution when consuming raw or undercooked foods, particularly seafood and meat dishes. Drink bottled water or boiled, filtered water to avoid waterborne illnesses, and use hand sanitizer before eating.

→ Allergy Management:

Be prepared for potential allergens commonly found in Japanese cuisine, such as soy, wheat, and seafood. Carry necessary medications, including antihistamines or epinephrine injectors, and learn to communicate your allergies in Japanese.

→ Chronic Health Conditions:

Ensure an adequate supply of prescription medications for the duration of your trip, along with a copy of your prescriptions and medical records. Research local medical facilities and pharmacies in advance for emergency refills or medical assistance.

→ Emergency Preparedness:

Familiarize yourself with emergency contact numbers, including local healthcare providers, ambulance services, and the nearest embassy or consulate for your country.

Keep a basic first aid kit and travel insurance information readily accessible for peace of mind during your journey.

By following these essential health precautions, you can minimize health risks and enjoy a safe and memorable trip to Japan.

CHAPTER 3

Landing in Japan: Arrival, Currency Exchange, Passports, and Visas

Welcome to Japan! In this third tip, we'll cover everything you need to know about arrival procedures, exchanging currency, and ensuring your passport and visa are in order. You will learn practical tips for a smooth arrival experience and navigating entry procedures effectively.

3.1 Arrival Procedures:

→ Customs and Immigration:

Upon arrival, proceed to the designated immigration counters for passport inspection and visa verification. Complete the required arrival forms accurately and have the necessary documents, including your passport, visa, and arrival card, readily available for inspection.

→ Baggage Claim:

After clearing immigration, proceed to the baggage claim area to retrieve your checked luggage. Verify baggage tags and collect your belongings from the designated carousel corresponding to your flight number.

→ Cultural Norms:

Respect local customs and cultural norms while in airports. Practice patience and courtesy when queueing, maintain a quiet demeanor in public areas, and be mindful of personal space. Learn basic Japanese phrases for communication and express gratitude for assistance from airport staff.

→ Transportation Options:

Upon exiting the baggage claim area, consider your transportation options to your destination. Airport trains, buses, and taxis are readily available and offer convenient transfers to city centers and other locations.

→ Navigating Airports:

Take note of airport layouts and directional signage to navigate terminals efficiently. Look out for signs indicating transportation hubs, baggage claim areas, and exit points. Adhere to airport rules and regulations, including security checkpoints and restrictions on certain items.

By following these arrival procedures and tips, you'll smoothly navigate Japan's airports and kickstart your adventure in the Land of the Rising Sun with confidence.

3.2 Currency Exchange:

→ Research Exchange Rates:

Research current exchange rates between your home currency and the Japanese yen. Trustworthy financial websites like XE.com or OANDA.com provide up-to-date exchange rate information that helps you plan your currency exchange strategy.

→ When to Exchange Currency:

Consider exchanging small cash for immediate needs before departing to Japan. However, for larger amounts, it's often more advantageous to exchange currency upon arrival in Japan.

→ Exchange at Arrival:

While airports offer currency exchange services for convenience, they typically have less favorable rates and higher fees. Instead, exchange only a small amount of cash at the airport for immediate needs and seek better rates at other locations in Japan.

→ Utilize ATMs:

Opt for ATMs operated by major banks or international networks such as Japan Post, Seven Bank, or convenience stores like 7-Eleven and FamilyMart once you arrive in Japan. These ATMs often offer competitive rates and may have English language options for easy navigation.

→ Notify Your Bank:

Inform your bank of your travel plans to Japan before departure. This prevents your bank from flagging overseas transactions as suspicious and ensures uninterrupted access to your funds while abroad.

→ Use Credit Cards Wisely:

Credit cards are widely accepted in Japan, especially in urban areas and tourist hubs. Look for credit cards with no foreign transaction fees or low exchange rate markups. Websites like NerdWallet.com or ThePointsGuy.com can help you compare credit card offers.

→ Carry Sufficient Cash:

While credit cards are convenient, not all establishments accept them, especially in rural or remote areas. Ensure you have enough cash on hand for purchases by planning.

→ Plan for Remote Areas:

If your itinerary includes remote destinations, research ATM availability, and banking facilities in advance. Reliable travel websites like JapanTravel.com or TripAdvisor.com can help you plan cash withdrawals and currency exchange in less accessible areas.

By utilizing reliable financial websites and travel resources, you can effectively manage your currency exchange and ensure seamless access to Japanese yen throughout your travels in Japan.

3.3 Passport Control :

→ Required Documentation:

Ensure you have a valid passport with at least six months of validity beyond your intended stay in Japan. Additionally, check visa requirements based on your nationality. Most visitors from countries like the United States, Canada, Australia, and many European nations can enter Japan for tourism or business purposes without a visa for up to 90 days.

→ Customs Declarations:

Complete a customs declaration form before arrival, accurately declaring any items subject to customs regulations, including cash exceeding ¥1,000,000 or restricted goods such as firearms, narcotics, or endangered species products. Familiarize yourself with Japan's customs regulations to avoid delays or penalties.

→ Common Pitfalls:

Avoid common pitfalls such as overstaying your visa or attempting to bring prohibited items into Japan. Be honest and transparent during customs inspections to avoid fines, deportation, or future travel restrictions.

→ Strategies for Expedited Processing:

Expedite your entry process by ensuring all required documentation is organized and easily accessible. Have a printed copy of your accommodation reservation and return flight itinerary in hand, as immigration officers may request these details.

→ Additional Regulations:

Stay informed about any additional regulations or health protocols implemented by Japanese authorities, especially during times of heightened security or public health concerns. Check official government websites or contact the nearest Japanese embassy or consulate for the latest information.

By following this concise checklist and adhering to Japanese immigration and customs regulations, travelers can ensure smooth entry into Japan and start their journey with confidence and peace of mind.

3.4 Visa Requirements :

→ Understanding Visa Categories:

Familiarize yourself with the different visa categories available for entry into Japan, including tourist visas, business visas, work visas, and long-term stay visas. Determine which visa category applies to your travel purpose and duration of stay.

→ Eligibility Criteria:

Check the eligibility criteria for each visa category to ensure you meet the requirements set by the Japanese government. This may include proof of sufficient funds, accommodation arrangements, travel itinerary, and health insurance coverage.

→ Application Process:

Research the visa application process specific to your country of residence. Visit the official website of the nearest Japanese embassy or consulate to access visa application forms, guidelines, and instructions. Ensure you submit all required documents accurately and within the specified timeframe.

→ Documentation Requirements:

Prepare the necessary documentation for your visa application, which may include a valid passport, passport-sized photos, visa application form, travel itinerary, proof of accommodation, financial statements, and any additional supporting documents as per the visa category.

→ Visa Fees:

Be aware of the visa application fees applicable to your visa category and nationality. Check the official website of the Japanese embassy or consulate for information on visa fees, payment methods, and any additional service charges.

→ Exemptions and Special Considerations:

Some nationalities may be exempt from visa requirements or eligible for visa exemptions under certain circumstances, such as short-term tourism or transit. Check the official website of the Japanese Ministry of Foreign Affairs for information on visa exemptions and special considerations based on nationality.

→ Processing Time:

Plan your visa application well in advance to account for processing times. Visa processing times may vary depending on your location, time of year, and visa category. Allow sufficient time for processing and consider expedited processing options if available.

→ Visa Validity and Duration of Stay:

Upon receiving your visa, review the validity period and duration of stay permitted. Ensure you adhere to the conditions of your visa, including entry and exit dates, maximum length of stay, and any visa restrictions or limitations.

→ Consultation and Assistance:

If you have any questions or concerns regarding visa requirements or the application process, contact the nearest Japanese embassy or consulate for assistance. Embassy staff can provide guidance and clarification on visa-related matters.

By understanding the visa requirements and following the necessary procedures, you can ensure a seamless entry into Japan, allowing you to focus on enjoying your travel experience in this fascinating destination.

CHAPTER 4

Finding Accommodations: Navigating Hotels, Ryokans, and More

Now that you're in Japan, and our fourth tip will guide you through the diverse landscape of accommodations, from luxury hotels to traditional ryokans and everything in between. You will learn about different lodging options, including hotels and traditional ryokans, and gain practical tips for navigating the booking process to find the perfect stay for your trip.

4.1 Accommodation Types

Welcome to Japan, where accommodation options are as diverse as the country's rich culture and traditions! Let's embark on a journey to discover some of the most unique places to lay your head:

→ Ryokans: The Zen Oasis

Approximate Price Range: **¥10,000 - ¥30,000 per night**

Picture yourself lounging on a futon, sipping green tea, and soaking in a serene hot spring bath. Ryokans are your ticket to traditional Japanese hospitality, complete with tatami mats, sliding doors, and delicious multi-course meals. It's like stepping into a tranquil oasis amidst the bustling cityscape!

→ Hotels: Where Comfort Meets Convenience

Approximate Price Range: **¥8,000 - ¥25,000 per night**

Need a soft bed, hot shower, and room service at your beck and call? Look no further than Japan's hotels! From sleek skyscrapers to cozy boutique inns, there's a hotel for every taste and budget. Plus, with additional amenities like Wi-Fi, breakfast buffets, and fluffy robes, you'll feel pampered from check-in to check-out.

→ Capsule Hotels: A Cozy Cocoon

Approximate Price Range: **¥2,000 - ¥5,000 per night**

Ever dreamed of sleeping in a futuristic pod straight out of a sci-fi movie? Capsule hotels make it a reality! Snuggle up in your little cocoon for the night, complete with a comfy mattress, personal TV, and maybe even a built-in massage chair. It's like your own private space capsule, ready for launch into dreamland!

→ Temple Stays: Zen and the Art of Lodging

Approximate Price Range: **Donation-based or ¥5,000 - ¥15,000 per night**

Seeking inner peace and spiritual enlightenment? Dive into the world of temple stays! Spend a night among the monks, practicing meditation, attending morning prayers, and savoring simple yet delicious vegetarian meals. It's a chance to disconnect from the chaos of modern life and reconnect with your inner zen master.

→ Themed Rooms: Where Fantasy Meets Reality

Approximate Price Range: **¥5,000 - ¥20,000 per night**

Ready for a stay that's out of this world? Step into a themed room and let your imagination run wild! From Hello Kitty wonderlands to traditional tea ceremonies, themed accommodations offer a quirky twist on the typical hotel experience. Who knows, you might even find yourself sleeping in a giant robot or in a giant sushi roll!

With these quirky accommodation options, your stay in Japan is bound to be a memorable adventure filled with laughter, relaxation, and maybe even a few surprises along the way. So pack your sense of humor and get ready to unlock Japan's hidden gems, one whimsical stay at a time!

4.2 Choosing The Right Accommodation Location

Selecting the perfect place to stay in Japan can elevate your travel experience to new heights. Here's how to find your dream accommodation:

- **Location Insights:** Imagine what matters most to you - being close to attractions, transportation, or dining options. Explore central hubs like Tokyo's bustling districts or opt for serene neighborhoods in Kyoto for a more tranquil stay.

- **Budget-Friendly Options:** Set a clear budget range and explore accommodation options within your financial comfort zone. Keep in mind the additional costs like taxes and fees, ensuring you stay within your overall travel budget.

- **Amenities Tailored to You:** Identify the must-have amenities that enhance your stay. Whether it's free Wi-Fi, complimentary breakfast, or convenient laundry facilities, prioritize what matters most to you.

- **Immerse Yourself in Culture:** Immerse yourself in Japan's rich culture by choosing accommodations that offer unique experiences. Consider a traditional ryokan for authentic Japanese hospitality or a temple stay for a serene escape.

- **Tap into Reviews and Recommendations:** Dive into online reviews and ratings to get insights from fellow travelers. Look for consistent positive feedback on cleanliness, staff friendliness, and overall satisfaction to make an informed decision.

By following these practical steps and customizing your accommodation choice to match your preferences and travel goals, you'll set the stage for an unforgettable adventure in Japan. Whether you're seeking urban excitement or rural tranquility, let your accommodation be the perfect launchpad for your Japanese journey.

4.3 Booking Methods

When it comes to booking accommodations in Japan, you're spoiled for choice with various methods to explore. Let's dive into your options:

First, online platforms like Booking.com, Airbnb, and Agoda are your go-to spots for a vast array of choices, from traditional ryokans to sleek modern hotels. These platforms let you filter your search by price, location, and amenities, and finally don't forget to read user reviews for insider tips.

If you prefer a more direct approach, many hotels in Japan allow you to book directly through their websites or by phone. Sometimes, this can even score exclusive deals or loyalty rewards, so it's worth checking out their offers.

For those who prefer a hands-off approach, travel agencies can be a lifesaver. They'll handle all the nitty-gritty details as part of a comprehensive travel package, ensuring everything is sorted for you.

But don't overlook local booking services, especially if you're venturing off the beaten path or looking for unique experiences like temple stays. These folks have insider knowledge and can offer personalized recommendations to make your stay extra special.

When booking, pay attention to payment options and cancellation policies. Some platforms require upfront payment, while others offer flexibility with cancellations. And keep your eyes peeled for deals and discounts – booking in advance often means better rates, but last-minute bargains can be found if you're flexible.

With these options at your disposal, finding the perfect accommodation for your Japan adventure becomes an interactive journey itself. Whether you're scrolling through online platforms or chatting with local booking services, each method offers its own unique experience to enhance your stay.

4.4 Ryokan Stay Advice

When comes to experiencing traditional Japanese hospitality, staying in a ryokan is a must-do for any traveler. Here's some advice to make the most of your ryokan experience:

Ryokan Stay

- **Research and Book Early:** Ryokans can book quickly, especially during peak seasons like cherry blossom or autumn foliage. Research different ryokans in your desired location and book well in advance to secure your preferred dates and room type.

- **Understand the Ryokan Experience:** Ryokans offer a unique blend of traditional Japanese accommodation, complete with tatami-mat floors, futon beds, and communal baths. Embrace the cultural experience by familiarizing yourself with ryokan etiquette, such as removing shoes at the entrance and wearing the provided yukata robe.

- **Choose Your Meal Plan:** Many Ryokans offer traditional kaiseki meals as part of your stay, featuring multi-course dining experiences showcasing seasonal ingredients. Decide whether you want to include meals in your reservation or opt for room-only accommodations.

- **Enjoy the Onsen Experience:** One of the highlights of staying at a ryokan is soaking in the rejuvenating waters of an onsen (hot spring). Be sure to follow proper etiquette when using the onsen, such as washing thoroughly before entering and refraining from bringing towels into the water.

- **Explore the Surroundings:** Ryokans are often situated in scenic locations, offering opportunities for nature walks, cultural excursions, and relaxation. Take advantage of the surroundings by exploring nearby attractions or simply unwinding in the tranquil setting of the Ryokan.

- **Communicate Your Preferences:** Don't hesitate to communicate any special requests or dietary restrictions to the Ryokan staff in advance. They are usually accommodating and will do their best to ensure you have a comfortable and enjoyable stay.

- **Respect Quiet Hours:** Ryokans prioritize tranquility and relaxation, so be mindful of noise levels, especially during designated quiet hours. Respect the peaceful atmosphere and fellow guests by keeping noise to a minimum, particularly in shared spaces like corridors and dining areas.

By following these tips, you can fully immerse yourself in the traditional charm and hospitality of a ryokan stay, creating unforgettable memories of your time in Japan.

CHAPTER 5

Getting Around: Transportation Essentials in Japan

Embark on a journey through Japan with confidence as our fifth tip "Getting Around: Transportation Essentials In Japan" breaks down the transportation essentials, ensuring you can navigate like a local from day one." Here you will learn about the various modes of transportation available, including trains, buses, and subways, and how to use them efficiently within Japan.

5.1 Train System Overview

Japan's extensive rail network offers travelers a convenient and comfortable way to explore the country. Whether you're zipping through the countryside on a sleek shinkansen or meandering along scenic coastal routes, trains provide an immersive and efficient travel experience. The costs of train travel in Japan can vary depending on factors like distance, train type, and whether you opt for individual tickets or a rail pass. For example, a one-way ticket on the Shinkansen between Tokyo and Kyoto can cost around ¥13,000 to ¥14,000 (approximately $120 to $130) for a standard reserved seat, while a 7-day JR Pass, which offers unlimited travel on JR trains, costs ¥29,110 (approximately USD 270) for ordinary class. Additional fees may apply for seat reservations and certain express trains, so it's essential to research your options and plan your budget accordingly.

Japan's rail system features diverse train types to suit different travel needs. The iconic Shinkansen offers high-speed travel between major cities, on the other hand, regional express trains connect cities and towns around the country. Local lines provide access to remote destinations and hidden gems, allowing travelers to explore Japan's diverse landscapes.

With an extensive network of rail lines, Japan offers endless possibilities for exploration. From bustling metropolises to tranquil countryside villages, there's a train route to suit every itinerary. Key routes connect major cities like Tokyo, Kyoto, and Osaka, making it easy to navigate between popular destinations.

Train System

Planning train travel in Japan is straightforward with various ticketing options available. The Japan Rail Pass (JR Pass) is a cost-effective choice for unlimited travel on JR trains, on the other hand, individual tickets are ideal for specific routes. Regional rail passes offer flexibility for localized travel, allowing travelers to tailor their journey to their preferences.

To make the most of your train travel experience, familiarize yourself with train station layouts and signage. Pay attention to announcements and allow extra time for transfers between trains. Consider purchasing a prepaid IC card for convenient fare payments and use smartphone apps to check train schedules and plan your journey.

Whether you're exploring Japan's vibrant cities or scenic countryside, the country's rail network provides a convenient and immersive way to discover its rich culture and natural beauty. So hop aboard, relax, and enjoy the ride as you embark on an unforgettable railway adventure across the Land of the Rising Sun.

5.2 Bus Routes

The country's bus system encompasses a wide array of routes catering to both urban commuters and leisure travelers. Major cities like Tokyo, Kyoto, and Osaka boast extensive bus networks, with routes covering key landmarks, shopping districts, and residential areas. In rural areas, local buses serve as vital lifelines, connecting remote communities and providing essential transportation for residents and visitors alike. Here is an extensive bus route from Tokyo to Kyoto and Osaka, Hokkaido to Hiroshima, Nagoya to Onsen.

→ Tokyo to Kyoto and Osaka:

- **Route:** The journey begins in Tokyo, the bustling capital of Japan, and heads southwest towards Kyoto and Osaka, two historic cities renowned for their cultural heritage and vibrant urban scenes.
- **Bus Services:** Express buses operated by reputable companies like Willer Express and JR Bus Kanto provide comfortable and efficient transportation between Tokyo, Kyoto, and Osaka, with multiple departures throughout the day.
- **Travel Time:** The journey typically takes around 6-8 hours, depending on traffic conditions and the specific bus route chosen.
- **Fare:** Prices for one-way bus tickets vary depending on the operator and the type of service, with fares typically ranging from ¥3,000 to ¥6,000 ($27 to $54).

→ Hokkaido to Hiroshima:

- **Route:** This scenic route spans the length of Japan, connecting the northern island of Hokkaido to the historic city of Hiroshima in the southwest.
- **Bus Services:** Several long-distance bus companies operate routes between Hokkaido and Hiroshima, offering comfortable coaches equipped with addi-

tional amenities such as reclining seats, onboard restrooms, and complimentary Wi-Fi.

- **Travel Time:** The journey covers approximately 1,200 kilometers and takes around 18-20 hours, including rest stops and transfers along the way.
- **Fare:** Prices for one-way bus tickets vary depending on the operator, route, and travel class, with fares typically ranging from ¥10,000 to ¥15,000 ($90 to $135).

→ Nagoya to Onsen:

- **Route:** Departing from Nagoya, a major transportation hub in central Japan, this route travels eastward towards scenic hot spring resorts known as onsen towns, nestled amidst the mountains and valleys of the Japanese countryside.
- **Bus Services:** Local bus companies operate routes between Nagoya and popular onsen destinations such as Gero Onsen, Shirahama Onsen, and Kinosaki Onsen, offering convenient transportation options for visitors seeking a tranquil retreat.
- **Travel Time:** The journey duration varies depending on the specific onsen town chosen, with travel times ranging from 2 to 4 hours.
- **Fare:** Prices for one-way bus tickets depend on the distance traveled and the operator, with fares typically ranging from ¥2,000 to ¥5,000 ($18 to $45).

By designing a road map that highlights key routes, highlights, bus services, travel times, and fares, you can easily plan your journeys and explore Japan's diverse landscapes, cultural attractions, and natural wonders.

5.3 Subway Systems

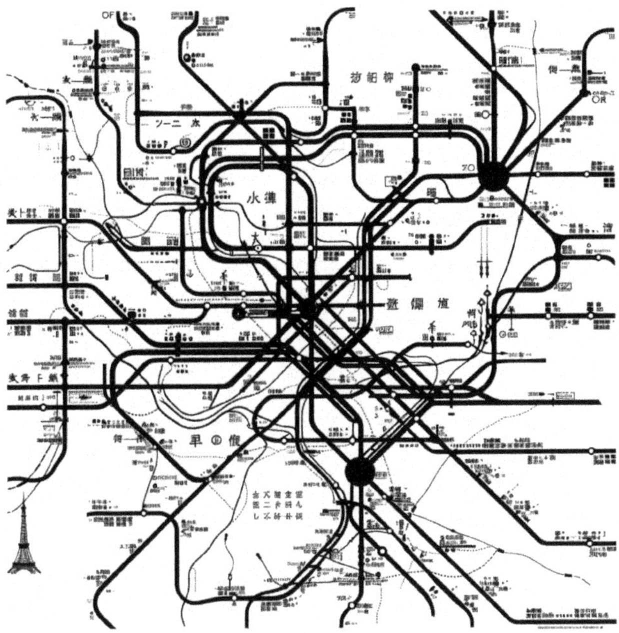

Subway Systems

Navigating Japan's subway systems can seem daunting at first, but with a little bit of preparation, you'll find it's a breeze. Let's dive into the key lines, stations, transfer points, fare structures, and useful tips to make your urban transit experience smooth and efficient.

Key Lines and Stations:

Ready to explore Tokyo, Osaka, and Kyoto? Let's start with Tokyo. The Yamanote Line circles the city, connecting major districts like Shibuya, Shinjuku, and Ueno. It's a must for first-time visitors. Don't forget the Ginza Line, which takes you through central Tokyo, hitting iconic areas such as Asakusa and Ginza. Heading to Osaka? The Midosuji Line is your north-south route, linking popular spots like Umeda, Namba, and Tennoji.

In Kyoto, the Karasuma Line is your go-to for reaching major attractions like Kyoto Station and the Imperial Palace.

Transfer Points:

Tokyo is a hub of activity, with Shinjuku Station being the busiest railway station in the world. Here, you can switch between multiple lines with ease. Tokyo Station is another critical hub, especially if you're catching a Shinkansen (bullet train). In Osaka, Umeda Station and Namba Station are key transfer points, connecting various subway, train, and bus lines. Kyoto Station is your main transfer hub in Kyoto, seamlessly linking local subway lines with regional and Shinkansen services.

Fare Structures:

Fares are based on distance traveled. In Tokyo, a short trip might cost around ¥170-¥200, while longer journeys can go up to ¥320 or more. The fare structure in Osaka and Kyoto is similar. To make things easier, get a rechargeable IC card like Suica or Pasmo. These cards can be used on subways, buses, and even for small purchases at convenience stores. Plus, they offer slightly discounted fares compared to single tickets.

By keeping these tips in mind, you'll be navigating Japan's subway systems like a pro. Enjoy your travels and make the most of your urban adventures!

5.4 Taxi Services

Navigating Japan's taxi systems can greatly enhance your travel experience, offering a convenient and reliable way to get around. Let's dive into everything you need to know to hail a cab and to your destination smoothly.

How to Hail a Taxi:

In Japan, it's quite straightforward. Look for taxis with a red-lit sign on the dashboard—this means the cab is available. If the sign is green, the taxi is occupied. In busy areas, such as near train stations or popular tourist spots, taxis are plentiful. Just raise your hand, and one will pull over.

Fare Structures:

Japanese taxis generally start at around ¥500 to ¥700 for the first few kilometers, with additional charges for every kilometer thereafter. Late-night rides (typically from 10 PM to 5 AM) might have a slight surcharge, so it's good to be prepared for a small increase if you're traveling during these hours. Taxis are metered, so you won't have to haggle over the price.

Payment Methods:

When coming to payment terms, most taxis accept cash and many now accept credit cards and IC cards (like Suica or Pasmo). It's always a good idea to confirm with the driver before your ride starts. Larger cities are more likely to have taxis equipped with card readers, but in rural areas, having cash on hand is advisable.

Concerned about the language barrier?

Here's a tip: have your destination written down in Japanese, or show the address on your smartphone. Many taxi drivers do not speak English but they are familiar with using GPS. Mentioning landmarks near your destination can also be helpful.

Want to make your ride even smoother?

Tipping is not customary in Japan, so don't worry about adding a gratuity. Also, note that taxi doors open and close automatically, so let the driver handle that for you. Lastly, if you're traveling with large luggage, check for taxis that have more space or consider using a taxi van service.

By understanding Japan's taxi system, you'll navigate your way around the cities with ease and confidence. Enjoy your rides!

5.5 Bicycle Rentals

Embark on a cycling adventure through Japan's captivating landscapes and vibrant cities. Get ready to pedal your way to unforgettable experiences with our comprehensive guide to bicycle rentals in Japan.

Finding Your Wheels:

Get started by locating the perfect rental spot. Whether you're in bustling Tokyo, historic Kyoto, or charming Osaka, rental shops are conveniently scattered throughout these cities. Keep an eye out for rental stations near major attractions, train stations, and even your accommodation. Don't forget to check with your hotel or hostel – many offer bike rentals as well. Plus, services like Docomo Bike Share and Kyoto Cycling Tour Project make renting a breeze with multiple locations and easy returns.

Budget-Friendly Rates:

Renting a bike in Japan won't break the bank. Typically, expect to pay around ¥1,000 to ¥1,500 per day for a standard bike. If you're planning an extended exploration, weekly rates are often available at discounted prices. And if you're up for an electric adventure, electric bikes are an option, usually priced at ¥2,500 to ¥3,500 per day.

Riding Safe and Sound:

Safety first, adventurers! Japan has cycling regulations in place to ensure your ride is smooth and secure. Always ride on the left side of the road, following traffic signals and signs. While helmets aren't mandatory for adults, they're recommended, especially for younger riders. Keep an eye out for designated bike lanes, especially in bustling urban areas, and remember to use bike lights at night for added visibility.

Scenic Routes and Hidden Gems:

Japan boasts a plethora of picturesque cycling paths waiting to be explored. In Tokyo, cruise along the Arakawa River or take in the sights around the Imperial Palace. Kyoto's Philosopher's Path and the Arashiyama Bamboo Grove offer serene settings for a leisurely ride. For the adventurous souls, the Shimanami Kaido route delivers stunning views of the Seto Inland Sea from island to island.

Urban and Rural Cycling Tips: Navigating city streets or countryside roads

Whether you're weaving through Tokyo's bustling neighborhoods or pedaling along rural paths, there are a few tips to remember. Always lock your bike when parked, stay hydrated, and carry a map or GPS for navigation. In rural areas, be mindful of narrow roads and local wildlife – and don't forget to take in the breathtaking scenery along the way.

Embark on a cycling journey through Japan and uncover its beauty and charm from a unique perspective. With our guide, you're ready to hop on a bike, explore with confidence, and create unforgettable memories on two wheels!

Chapter 6

Exploring Tokyo: Embracing the Heartbeat of Japan's Capital

Our sixth tip invites you to dive deep into Tokyo, a city where tradition meets ultramodern in the most captivating ways. The chapter "Exploring Tokyo: Japan's Dynamic Capital" offers you practical guidance and insights for navigating Tokyo's bustling streets, vibrant culture, and iconic landmarks. You will discover essential travel tips and recommendations for uncovering the unique charms of Japan's capital city.

6.1 Iconic Landmarks

Tokyo is a city of contrasts, where ultramodern skyscrapers coexist with historic temples. Here's your ultimate guide to some of the city's most iconic landmarks, with descriptions, historical significance, visiting tips, and nearby attractions. Let's dive in!

Tokyo Tower in Spring

→ Tokyo Tower:

First up, we have Tokyo Tower. Imagine the Eiffel Tower, but taller and painted in bright orange and white. Standing at 333 meters, Tokyo Tower offers breathtaking views of the city.

- **Historical Significance:** Tokyo Tower isn't just for looks. Completed in 1958, it symbolizes Japan's post-war rebirth and modernization. Pretty cool, right?
- **Visiting Tips:** Here's a tip: Arrive early to beat the crowds. Consider visiting both the Main Deck and the Top Deck for different perspectives. And don't miss the glass-floor sections if you're brave enough to look straight down!
- **Nearby Attractions:** After soaking in the views, take a short walk to Zojo-ji Temple for a serene contrast to the bustling cityscape. It's the perfect way to balance your day.

→ Senso-ji Temple:

Next, let's head to Senso-ji in Asakusa, Tokyo's oldest temple. Picture the striking red Kaminarimon (Thunder Gate) with its giant lantern—it's a sight you won't forget.

- **Historical Significance:** Founded in 645 AD, Senso-ji has stood the test of time as a significant spiritual site. Imagine all the history those walls have seen!
- **Visiting Tips:** To avoid the crowds, visit early in the morning or late in the evening. Don't forget to explore Nakamise Shopping Street leading up to the temple. It's a great spot for traditional snacks and souvenirs.
- **Nearby Attractions:** After your temple visit, wander around Asakusa's traditional entertainment district. For a unique view of the city, consider taking a boat ride on the Sumida River.

→ Shibuya Crossing: Ready for some urban energy?

Shibuya Crossing is known as the world's busiest pedestrian crossing. It's a dynamic display of Tokyo's fast-paced lifestyle.

- **Historical Significance:** Shibuya Crossing has become a symbol of modern Tokyo. Think of it as the heartbeat of the city, connecting people from all walks of life.
- **Visiting Tips:** For the best views, head to the second floor of the Starbucks in the QFRONT building or check out the new Shibuya Scramble Square observation deck.
- **Nearby Attractions:** After the crossing, dive into Shibuya's fashion-forward shops. Don't miss the statue of Hachiko, the loyal dog, right outside Shibuya Station. It's a heartwarming sight.

→ The Imperial Palace:

Imperial Palace in Winter

Last but not least, let's visit the Imperial Palace, home to Japan's Emperor. The palace is surrounded by beautiful gardens and moats. While the inner grounds are usually closed to the public, the East Gardens are open and free to visit.

Historical Significance: Built on the site of the old Edo Castle, the palace grounds hold significant historical and cultural importance. It's like stepping back in time.

- **Visiting Tips:** Remember, the East Gardens are closed on Mondays and Fridays, so plan your visit accordingly. Joining a guided tour can offer deeper insights into the site's rich history.
- **Nearby Attractions:** Take a stroll through the nearby Marunouchi district, known for its upscale shopping and dining options. Or, visit the National Museum of Modern Art for a cultural treat.

Planning Your Itinerary:

When planning your Tokyo itinerary, try to group these landmarks by their proximity to each other to make the most of your time. For example, visit Tokyo Tower and Zojo-ji Temple on the same day, or combine a trip to Senso-ji Temple with a visit to the nearby Sumida River and Asakusa district.

By exploring these iconic landmarks, you'll experience both the traditional and modern sides of Tokyo, ensuring a well-rounded and unforgettable adventure in Japan's capital city. Ready to explore? Let's go!

6.2 Neighborhoods to Explore

Tokyo is a city of diverse neighborhoods, each offering its unique blend of attractions, dining options, shopping experiences, and cultural highlights. Ready to explore? Let's dive into some must-visit neighborhoods in Tokyo, including Shinjuku, Asakusa, and Harajuku!

→ Shinjuku: The City That Never Sleeps

- **Unique Attractions:** Shinjuku is the epitome of urban excitement. Start your adventure at the Tokyo Metropolitan Government Building for a panoramic view of the city from its observation decks—an unbeatable free experience.

Don't miss the vibrant nightlife in Kabukicho, Tokyo's famous entertainment district, where neon lights and bustling streets create an electrifying atmosphere.

- **Dining Options:** Foodies, rejoice! Shinjuku offers a culinary journey like no other. For an unforgettable dining experience, visit Omoide Yokocho, also known as "Memory Lane," where tiny alleyways are packed with izakayas (Japanese pubs) serving delicious yakitori (grilled chicken skewers) and other traditional snacks. Looking for something a bit more upscale? Try the luxurious restaurants in the Shinjuku Park Tower.

- **Shopping Experiences:** Shinjuku is a shopping haven. The area around Shinjuku Station is filled with department stores like Isetan and Takashimaya, where you can find everything from high-end fashion to local crafts. For electronics, the Yodobashi Camera is a must-visit.

- **Cultural Highlights:** Take a peaceful break from the urban chaos at Shinjuku Gyoen National Garden, a beautiful green oasis perfect for a stroll. The garden is especially stunning during cherry blossom season.

→ Asakusa: A Glimpse into Old Tokyo

Asakusa - Old Tokyo

Unique Attractions: Step back in time in Asakusa, home to the iconic Senso-ji Temple, Tokyo's oldest and most significant temple. The Kaminarimon Gate, with its giant red lantern, is a popular photo spot. Walk through Nakamise Shopping Street, lined with stalls selling traditional snacks and souvenirs, leading up to the temple.

- **Dining Options:** Asakusa is a paradise for those seeking traditional Japanese cuisine. Try tempura at Daikokuya or savor some delicious soba (buckwheat noodles) at Namiki Yabusoba. Don't forget to sample taiyaki, a fish-shaped cake filled with sweet red bean paste, from one of the street vendors.

- **Shopping Experiences:** Nakamise Shopping Street isn't the only place to shop in Asakusa. Explore the side streets and discover charming shops selling everything from kimono fabrics to traditional crafts. For a unique experience, visit Kappabashi Street, also known as "Kitchen Town," where you can find a plethora of kitchenware and fake food displays.
- **Cultural Highlights:** Immerse yourself in the rich cultural heritage of Asakusa. Take a leisurely rickshaw ride to explore the area traditionally. Visit the Asakusa Culture and Tourist Information Center for a stunning view of the neighborhood from its observation deck.

→ Harajuku: The Heart of Youth Culture and Fashion

- **Unique Attractions:** Harajuku is synonymous with cutting-edge fashion and youth culture. Start your visit at Takeshita Street, the epicenter of teenage culture, filled with quirky shops, trendy boutiques, and colorful cafes. Nearby, Omotesando Avenue offers a more upscale shopping experience with luxury brands and sophisticated architecture.
- **Dining Options:** Harajuku is famous for its creative and Instagram-worthy treats. Try the rainbow-colored cotton candy or crepes filled with all sorts of sweet delights. For a more substantial meal, visit one of the chic cafes or restaurants along Omotesando Avenue.
- **Shopping Experiences:** Shop till you drop in Harajuku. Takeshita Street is the place to find the latest in youth fashion, on the other hand, Omotesando Avenue caters to those with a taste for high-end brands. Don't miss the unique boutiques in the backstreets, where you can find one-of-a-kind fashion pieces and accessories.
- **Cultural Highlights:** Take a break from shopping and visit the serene Meiji Shrine, located in a lush forested area just a short walk from the bustling streets

of Harajuku. It's a perfect spot to experience a bit of tranquility amidst the urban excitement.

Ready to Explore Tokyo's Neighborhoods?

Each of these neighborhoods offers a unique slice of Tokyo life, from the bustling energy of Shinjuku to the historic charm of Asakusa and the trendy vibe of Harajuku. Whether you're a foodie, a fashion enthusiast, or a culture buff, Tokyo's diverse neighborhoods have something special in store for you. So, lace up your walking shoes, grab your camera, and get ready to explore the multifaceted charm of this incredible city!

6.3 Cultural Experience

Tokyo is not just a modern metropolis; it's also a city deeply rooted in tradition and culture. To truly experience the essence of Japan, you need to immerse yourself in the diverse cultural activities available. Here's your guide to some unforgettable cultural experiences in Tokyo:

→ Tea Ceremonies:

Ever wondered what it's like to participate in a Japanese tea ceremony? It's much more than just drinking tea. Imagine yourself in a serene tea house like Hamarikyu Gardens, surrounded by tranquil beauty. The tea ceremony, or "chanoyu," is a meditative practice embodying harmony, respect, purity, and tranquility. Participate in a class and learn the meticulous process of making and serving matcha. You'll gain insights into the historical and cultural significance of each step, making it a memorable experience.

→ Sumo Wrestling Matches:

It's an exciting and unique way to connect with Japanese culture. Head to Tokyo's Ryogoku Kokugikan for the premier tournaments held in January, May, and September. If you're visiting outside these months, don't worry—you can still visit a sumo stable to watch the morning practice sessions. It's a fascinating glimpse into the lives and discipline of these powerful athletes.

→ Traditional Festivals:

Do you love festivals? Tokyo hosts numerous traditional festivals throughout the year, each offering a window into Japan's rich cultural tapestry. The Sanja Matsuri in Asakusa, held in May, features parades of portable shrines and traditional music. If you're here in spring, the cherry blossom season brings hanami (flower viewing) parties. Join locals in parks like Ueno and Shinjuku Gyoen to celebrate the blooming Sakura with food, drinks, and festivities.

→ Kimono Rentals:

Ever wanted to wear a kimono? For a truly immersive experience, rent a kimono for a day. Many shops in Asakusa and Harajuku offer packages with dressing assistance and hairstyling. Picture yourself strolling through historic neighborhoods, temples, and shrines in traditional attire. It's like stepping back in time, and it makes for fantastic photos. Plus, it's a wonderful way to feel connected to Japan's cultural heritage.

→Visits to Historical Sites:

Are you a history buff? Tokyo is home to numerous historical sites that offer insights into Japan's past. Senso-ji Temple in Asakusa, Tokyo's oldest temple, is a must-visit. Explore the sprawling grounds, traditional shops, and the iconic Kaminarimon Gate. Another gem is the Meiji Shrine, nestled in a lush forest near Harajuku, offering a serene escape from the city's hustle and bustle. And don't miss the Imperial Palace, where you can tour the East Gardens and learn about Japan's imperial history.

Making the Most of Your Cultural Experience:

Consider joining guided tours that provide deeper insights into the historical and cultural context of these activities. And don't hesitate to ask locals for recommendations—they often know about hidden gems and events that aren't widely advertised. Engaging with Tokyo's rich cultural offerings will undoubtedly enrich your trip and provide lasting memories. Enjoy your journey into the heart of Japan's culture!

6.4 Dining and Nightlife

Ready to dive into Tokyo's legendary dining and nightlife?

Buckle up! This city is a foodie's paradise and a night owl's dream come true. Here's your guide to navigating Tokyo's culinary delights and vibrant nightlife.

→ Top Restaurants:

Tokyo's dining scene is top-notch. If you're a sushi lover, Sukiyabashi Jiro or Sushi Saito will blow your mind with their Michelin-starred sushi experiences. Craving something hearty? Head to Ichiran or Ippudo, where the ramen is so good, that you might find yourself slurping down a second bowl without a second thought. Don't forget to try tempura at Tenmatsu or a traditional kaiseki meal at Ryugin – both are unforgettable.

→ Street Food Markets:

For a more casual bite, Tokyo's street food markets are where the action is. Tsukiji Outer Market is perfect for fresh seafood snacks, like grilled scallops or tuna skewers. If you're wandering around Asakusa, try the teriyaki (fish-shaped cakes filled with sweet red bean paste) and yakitori (grilled chicken skewers) at Nakamise Shopping Street. The atmosphere here is electric, and the food is to die for.

→ Izakayas and Themed Cafes:

Want a truly local experience? Visit an izakaya, like Ebisu Yokocho or Shinjuku Golden Gai, for some after-work drinks and small plates. These casual bars are great for mingling with locals over some sake and grilled snacks. For something quirky, Tokyo's themed cafes are unbeatable. Whether it's the magical ambiance of a Harry Potter cafe or the feline company at a cat cafe in Akihabara, there's a spot that will tickle your fancy.

→ Nightlife Spots:

As the sun sets, Tokyo's nightlife comes alive. Start your night at one of the city's many bars. For an unforgettable view, try the New York Bar at the Park Hyatt, famous for the movie "Lost in Translation." If you're into craft cocktails, Bar High Five in Ginza is a must-visit. Feeling like dancing? Head to Womb in Shibuya or ageHa in Shin-Kiba, where the beats keep you moving until the early hours. For a more laid-back vibe, Golden Gai's tiny, themed bars offer a unique experience with each door you open.

→ Entertainment Districts:

Tokyo's entertainment districts are buzzing with energy. In Shibuya, the iconic crossing is just the beginning – explore the neon-lit streets packed with clubs, bars, and late-night eateries. Roppongi is another hot spot for nightlife, known for its international crowd and upscale clubs. If you're into live music, Koenji and Shimokitazawa are the places to be, with numerous venues offering everything from jazz to punk.

Making the Most of Tokyo's Dining and Nightlife:

To fully enjoy Tokyo's dining and nightlife, plan your evenings and make reservations for popular spots. Don't be afraid to ask locals for recommendations; they often know the best-hidden gems. Whether you're indulging in gourmet cuisine, savoring street food, or dancing till dawn, Tokyo's culinary and social scenes promise an unforgettable experience. Enjoy every bite and every moment!

6.5 Practical Tips For Visitors

Tokyo is a vibrant city with so much to offer, but it can be overwhelming if you're not prepared. Let's dive into some practical tips to ensure your journey is smooth, enjoyable, and full of unforgettable moments.

→ Navigating Public Transportation:

Tokyo's public transportation is legendary for its efficiency, but it can be daunting for first-timers. Here's a pro tip: as soon as you land, grab a Suica or Pasmo card. These rechargeable smart cards make hopping on and off trains and buses a breeze. Trust me, it's a lifesaver. Also, download the Japan Transit Planner or Hyperdia app to help you navigate routes and schedules. And don't worry if you get lost – Tokyoites are generally friendly and willing to help.

→ Understanding Local Etiquette:

Japanese etiquette is fascinating and shows great respect for others. For instance, remember to bow slightly when greeting someone – it's a small gesture but goes a long way. When using escalators, stand on the left side and walk on the right. And here's a quirky one: avoid talking on your phone while on public transport. It's considered impolite, and you'll blend in much better if you follow this unspoken rule.

→ Managing Language Barriers:

While many signs are in English and you'll find English speakers in major tourist areas, learning a few basic phrases can be incredibly helpful and appreciated. Simple words like "Arigatou" (Thank you) and "Sumimasen" (Excuse me/I'm sorry) can make a big difference. Also, having a translation app like Google Translate can be a handy tool for those tricky moments.

→ Using Cash Versus Cards:

In Tokyo, cash is still king. Many places, especially smaller shops and restaurants, prefer cash over cards. Make sure to carry enough yen with you. ATMs in convenience stores like 7-Eleven and Lawson usually accept international cards, so you can withdraw cash easily. But don't worry – major stores, hotels, and restaurants will generally accept credit cards.

→ Accessing Wi-Fi and Essential Services:

Staying connected is crucial for navigating Tokyo. Pocket Wi-Fi is a popular choice for tourists and can be rented at the airport or booked online before you arrive. It provides a reliable internet connection for your devices wherever you go. Alternatively, look for free Wi-Fi hotspots in cafes, hotels, and major train stations. And don't forget to keep a portable charger handy – you'll be using your phone a lot!

By following these tips, you'll be well-prepared to tackle Tokyo like a pro. Whether you're exploring bustling markets, serene temples, or neon-lit streets, these insights will help you navigate the city with confidence and ease. Enjoy your adventure in Tokyo – it's going to be incredible!

CHAPTER 7

Discovering Kyoto and Osaka: Delving into Tradition and Excitement

Discover the heart of Japan with our seventh tip, guiding you through the historic wonders of Kyoto and the lively attractions of Osaka. The chapter "Discovering Kyoto and Osaka: Delving into Tradition and Vibrancy" guides you through the cultural richness and vibrant atmosphere of Kyoto and Osaka. Here, you will learn about the historical landmarks, traditional customs, and modern attractions that define these two iconic cities in Japan.

7.1 Kyoto's Famous Sights

Hey there, Ready to dive into the wonders of Kyoto, the ancient capital of Japan? Get set for a journey through history, culture, and some seriously stunning sights. Here's your ultimate guide to exploring Kyoto's most iconic landmarks.

→ Kinkaku-ji (The Golden Pavilion):

Kinkaku-ji (The Golden Pavilion) in Autumn

- **Historical Significance:** Ever heard of a temple covered in gold leaf? Welcome to Kinkaku-ji! This Zen Buddhist temple, built in the late 14th century, is as opulent as it gets.
- **Best Visiting Times:** Trust me, you'll want to get here right when it opens at 9:00 AM to beat the crowds. If you can, plan your visit during the fall for incredible foliage or in winter when the pavilion is beautifully dusted with snow.
- **Tips for Enhancing Your Visit:** Don't rush! Take a stroll through the gardens. The reflection of the pavilion on the pond is picture-perfect, so keep your camera ready. Oh! and there's a tea house inside – the matcha is a must-try!

→ Fushimi Inari Shrine:

Fushimi Inari Shrine

Historical Significance: Imagine walking through thousands of vermilion torii gates. That's Fushimi Inari Shrine, dedicated to the Shinto God of rice and agriculture. This place has been around since 711 AD!

Best Visiting Times: Early morning or late afternoon is your best bet to avoid the crowds. And if you can catch the sunset, you're in for a treat as the gates glow in the fading light.

- **Tips for Enhancing Your Visit:** Wear comfy shoes because the hike to the top of Mount Inari is long but worth it. Take your time and explore the smaller, quieter paths. The journey itself is an experience.

→ Arashiyama Bamboo Grove:

- **Historical Significance:** Walking through the Arashiyama Bamboo Grove feels like stepping into another world. The towering bamboo stalks create a serene and surreal atmosphere.
- **Best Visiting Times:** Get there at sunrise for a peaceful experience. Trust me, the early wake-up call is worth it!

Arashiyama Bamboo Grove

- **Tips for Enhancing Your Visit:** Pair your visit with a trip to Tenryu-ji Temple and the scenic Togetsukyo Bridge. Consider renting a bicycle to explore the area – it's a fun way to see more. And if you have time, check out the Iwatayama Monkey Park for great views of Kyoto and some monkey business.

Additional Tips for Your Kyoto Adventure:

- **Transportation:** Kyoto's bus system is super efficient. Grab a day pass for convenience, or rent a bike for a more immersive experience.
- **Cultural Etiquette:** Be respectful at religious sites. Dress modestly and pay attention to photography rules, especially inside temples.
- **Local Cuisine:** Kyoto's food scene is amazing! Don't miss out on kaiseki (traditional multi-course meal), yudofu (tofu hot pot), and matcha sweets. Nishiki Market is your go-to for sampling local delights.

So there you have it – a guide to soaking in the best of Kyoto. Follow this itinerary and you'll not only see the famous sights but also gain a deeper appreciation for their historical and cultural significance. Happy travels, and enjoy every moment in this timeless city!

7.2 Osaka's Exciting Places

Ready to dive into Osaka's vibrant mix of culture, history, and non-stop entertainment? Let's explore some of the most exciting spots this city has to offer. Here's your insider guide to Dotonbori, Osaka Castle, and Universal Studios Japan, complete with tips to make your visit unforgettable.

→ Dotonbori:

Welcome to the heart of Osaka's nightlife and culinary scene, where neon lights and tantalizing aromas fill the air.

- **Must-Try Street Foods:** You can't leave Dotonbori without trying takoyaki (octopus balls) and okonomiyaki (savory pancakes). Look for the giant mechanical crab at Kani Doraku; it's an iconic spot to grab some fresh crab dishes.

Dotonbori

Tips for Maximizing Fun: Head to Dotonbori after dark when the area truly comes alive. The illuminated signs and bustling atmosphere are mesmerizing. Don't miss taking a selfie with the famous Glico running man sign. Wander along the canal, and if you're feeling social, pop into a standing bar to chat with locals – it's a great way to soak up the local culture.

→ Osaka Castle:

Step back in time at Osaka Castle, symbolizing the city's rich history and resilience.

- **Historical Insights:** Built in the late 16th century by Toyotomi Hideyoshi, this castle played a pivotal role in the unification of Japan. The castle grounds and museum offer a deep dive into Japan's feudal era.
- **Tips for Maximizing Exploration:** Arrive early to avoid the crowds. The castle grounds are stunning, especially during cherry blossom season. Inside, the museum features fascinating samurai exhibits. Climb to the top-floor observation deck for panoramic city views. It's also worth exploring the surrounding Nishinomaru Garden for a serene escape.

→ Universal Studios Japan (USJ):

For a dose of thrills and movie magic, Universal Studios Japan is a must-visit.

- **Fun and Adventure:** USJ is home to incredible attractions and rides based on blockbuster films like Harry Potter, Jurassic Park, and Minions. It's perfect for families, thrill-seekers, and film buffs.
- **Tips for Maximizing Fun:** Buy your tickets online in advance to skip the

ents. For an unforgettable kaiseki experience, visit Kikunoi, a Michelin-starred restaurant where the culinary artistry will blow you away. Be sure to make a reservation well in advance to secure your spot at this gastronomic haven.

- **Nishiki Market:** Next, stroll through Nishiki Market, also known as "Kyoto's Kitchen." This bustling market is filled with stalls selling fresh seafood, seasonal produce, and local delicacies. Don't miss out on yuba (tofu skin), which is a Kyoto specialty. Try some samples as you wander the market, and pick up a few snacks for later. It's a great way to immerse yourself in the local food culture.

- **Matcha:** Everything Kyoto is famous for its matcha (green tea), and you'll find it in everything from drinks to desserts. Head to Tsujiri, a renowned tea shop, for a matcha parfait or matcha ice cream. The rich, earthy flavor of high-quality matcha is something you simply can't miss while in Kyoto.

→ Osaka: The Nation's Kitchen

- **Okonomiyaki:** Osaka's most famous dish, okonomiyaki, is a savory pancake filled with ingredients like cabbage, meat, and seafood, then topped with a variety of condiments. For the best okonomiyaki, head to Mizuno in the Dotonbori area. This family-run restaurant has been serving up delicious okonomiyaki for generations. Grab a seat at the counter and watch as the chefs skillfully prepare your meal right before your eyes.

- **Takoyaki:** Next, let's talk about takoyaki – those delightful octopus-filled balls of goodness. You'll find takoyaki stands all over Osaka, but for a real treat, visit Creo-ru in Dotonbori. These crispy-on-the-outside, gooey-on-the-inside snacks are perfect for a quick bite as you explore the city. Enjoy them hot off the grill, topped with savory sauce, mayo, and bonito flakes.

- **Kuromon Ichiba Market:** For a true taste of Osaka's food culture, visit Kuromon Ichiba Market. This lively market is famous for its fresh seafood and street food. Try grilled scallops, sea urchins, and other seafood delights. Don't forget to sample kushikatsu – deep-fried skewers of meat and vegetables. The variety and quality of food here are astounding, making it a must-visit for any food lover.

→ Dining Tips and Local Delicacies:

- **Reservation Tips:** For high-end dining experiences, such as kaiseki in Kyoto or popular restaurants in Osaka, making a reservation is essential. Many top dining spots fill up quickly, so plan and book your table early.
- **Seasonal Delicacies:** Japan's cuisine is deeply tied to the seasons, so be sure to try seasonal specialties. In spring, savor dishes made with fresh bamboo shoots; in summer, enjoy refreshing hamo (pike conger eel); autumn brings matsutake mushrooms; and winter is perfect for nabemono (hot pot) dishes.
- **Street Food Adventures:** Both Kyoto and Osaka have vibrant street food scenes. In Kyoto, explore the stalls at Arashiyama's Bamboo Grove and Fushimi Inari Shrine. In Osaka, Dotonbori and Shinsekai are your go-to spots for an array of tasty street food.

There you have it, food enthusiasts! Kyoto and Osaka offer a culinary adventure like no other, with each city providing its unique flavors and dining experiences. From traditional kaiseki to sizzling street food, your taste buds are in for a treat. So, grab your chopsticks, and let the food journey begin!

CHAPTER 8

Journeying to Hokkaido and Hiroshima: Experiencing Nature and History

Tip eight takes you from the serene beauty of Hokkaido's landscapes to the reflective memorials of Hiroshima, creating a journey rich in nature and history. The chapter "Journeying to Hokkaido and Hiroshima: Experiencing Nature and History" guides you through the distinct landscapes and historical narratives of Hokkaido and Hiroshima. You will explore Hokkaido's natural beauty and learn about Hiroshima's historical significance, gaining insights into the cultural and historical diversity of these regions in Japan.

8.1 Hokkaido's Natural Attractions & Cultural Landmarks

Hey there, adventure seekers! This northern island of Japan is a treasure trove of natural beauty and rich cultural history. From stunning national parks to charming historical villages, here's your comprehensive guide to Hokkaido's must-see attractions. Let's dive in!

→ Shikotsu-Toya National Park: Nature's Paradise

- **Scenic Beauty and Activities:** Picture this: you're kayaking on the crystal-clear waters of Lake Shikotsu, surrounded by lush greenery. Sounds amazing, right? Shikotsu-Toya National Park is an incredible blend of volcanic landscapes, serene lakes, and dense forests. If you're more into relaxing, Lake Toya is your spot, known for its soothing hot springs. And don't forget Mount Usu – an active volcano with jaw-dropping views from the top. Hop on the ropeway and hike around the crater for a truly memorable experience.
- **Best Time to Visit:** Spring and autumn is absolutely magical here. In spring, the park is a sea of cherry blossoms, while autumn transforms it into a canvas of vibrant foliage. Trust me, both seasons offer perfect weather for exploring.

→ The Blue Pond: A Picture-Perfect Marvel

- **Stunning Azure Waters:** Ever seen a pond so blue it looks like it's been photoshopped? Welcome to the Blue Pond in Biei! The pond's vibrant color comes from natural minerals, creating a surreal, almost magical landscape. Whether you're a pro photographer or just love snapping pics, this place is a must-visit. Each season brings its own charm: lush greens in summer, fiery reds and oranges in autumn, and serene snow-covered beauty in winter.
- **Tips for Visiting:** For the best photos, visit early in the morning or late in

the afternoon. And while you're there, don't miss the nearby Shirahige Falls – equally stunning!

→ Historic Village of Hokkaido: A Journey Through Time

Ready for a time-travel experience?

- **Cultural Immersion:** The Historic Village of Hokkaido takes you back to the Meiji and Taisho periods. Wander through traditional farmhouses, shops, and schools to get a feel for what life was like in Hokkaido over a century ago. They often host traditional crafts and cultural activities, so roll up your sleeves and get involved!

- **Best Season to Explore:** Honestly, this place is a delight year-round. Winter's snow-covered buildings look like something out of a fairy tale, on the other hand, while summer and autumn offer perfect weather for exploring and participating in outdoor activities.

→ Additional Tips for Your Hokkaido Adventure:

- **Seasonal Highlights:** Hokkaido is stunning all year round, but each season has its perks. Winter is perfect for skiing in Niseko or marveling at the Sapporo Snow Festival. Spring brings breathtaking cherry blossoms, summer is ideal for the flower fields in Furano, and autumn is great for hiking and enjoying the fall colors.

- **Local Cuisine:** You can't leave Hokkaido without indulging in its delicious food. Fresh seafood like crab, sea urchin, and salmon are must-tries. And don't miss the local ramen shops for some mouth-watering miso ramen, or the dairy products like cheese and ice cream – they're to die for!

- **Getting Around:** Hokkaido is vast, but well-connected by public transportation. For more flexibility, especially if you want to visit remote areas, renting a car is a great option.

So there you have it, intrepid explorers! Hokkaido is a land of contrasts, offering everything from tranquil lakes and volcanic landscapes to historic villages and modern cities. Each season brings its unique charm, so no matter when you visit, you're in for an unforgettable adventure. Pack your bags, bring your camera, and get ready to explore the wonders of Hokkaido!

8.2 Hiroshima's Historical Sites & Peace Memorials

Ready to step into a poignant part of history?

If Hiroshima is on your itinerary, you're in for a deeply moving experience. This city is a testament to resilience and a powerful symbol of peace. Let's explore Hiroshima's must-visit historical sites and peace memorials together. I'll share their significance and handy tips to ensure your visit is meaningful and memorable.

→ Hiroshima Peace Memorial Park: A Sanctuary of Reflection

- **Historical Significance:** Imagine walking through an area that was once a bustling city center, now transformed into a serene haven dedicated to peace. That's Hiroshima Peace Memorial Park for you. Created to honor the victims of the atomic bomb dropped on August 6, 1945, this park stands as a beacon for world peace and remembrance.
- **Visiting Highlights:**

1. ***Flame of Peace:*** Picture this: an eternal flame that symbolizes the world's yearning for peace. It will remain lit until nuclear weapons are abolished worldwide. Powerful, right?
2. ***Cenotaph for the A-bomb Victims:*** This arched tomb holds a registry of names of those who perished due to the bombing. When you stand before it, take a moment to reflect on the lives lost.

3. ***Children's Peace Monument:*** Have you heard of Sadako Sasaki and her thousand paper cranes? This monument, inspired by her story, is a touching tribute to the children who lost their lives.

4. ***Tips for a Meaningful Visit:*** Here's a tip: consider joining a guided tour to deepen your understanding of each monument. These tours can provide insights you might miss on your own. Also, visiting early in the morning or late in the afternoon often offers a more peaceful experience, away from the larger crowds.

→ Atomic Bomb Dome: A Testament to Resilience

- **Historical Significance:** Let's move on to the Atomic Bomb Dome, shall we? This iconic structure, once the Hiroshima Prefectural Industrial Promotion Hall, was one of the few buildings left standing near the bomb's hypocenter. Preserved in its post-explosion state, it serves as a stark reminder of the devastating impact of nuclear warfare and a call to prevent such destruction in the future.

- **Visiting Tips:** When you visit, try to imagine the sheer force that this building withstood. It's quite overwhelming. I recommend visiting at dusk when the dome is illuminated – it adds an extra layer of solemn beauty to your experience.

→ Hiroshima Peace Memorial Museum: An Emotional Journey

- **Historical Significance:** The Hiroshima Peace Memorial Museum offers an in-depth look at the events leading up to the bombing, the aftermath, and the human stories behind the statistics. It's both heartbreaking and inspiring.

- **Exhibit Highlights:**

1. ***Artifacts and Photographs:*** From tattered clothes to melted objects, these items bring the human cost of the bombing into sharp focus.

2. ***Survivor Stories:*** Personal accounts and testimonies from survivors, or hibakusha, are perhaps the most moving part of the museum.

- **Visiting Tips Pro tip:** Give yourself plenty of time to go through the exhibits. The content is heavy and can be emotionally taxing, so don't rush. If possible, attend one of the survivor talks – their stories are incredibly powerful and provide a perspective that no display can match.

Making the Most of Your Visit:

Respectful and Meaningful Visits: A few tips to wrap up: always approach these sites with the respect they deserve. Silence your phone, speak in hushed tones, and take your time to fully absorb the significance of each site. Consider leaving a paper crane at the Children's Peace Monument – it's a beautiful way to participate in the call for peace.

There you have it! Hiroshima's historical sites and peace memorials offer a profound, reflective experience that will stay with you long after your visit. Prepare yourself for an emotional journey and take away a deeper understanding of the importance of peace. Safe travels!

8.3 Culinary Delights in Hokkaido and Hiroshima

Hey there, food enthusiasts! Embark on a culinary adventure through Hokkaido and Hiroshima These regions are renowned for their unique and mouthwatering specialties. Let's dive into the delectable world of fresh seafood, dairy delights, and savory pancakes, and I'll guide you to the top spots where you can indulge in these local flavors. Get ready to tantalize your taste buds!

→ Hokkaido: A Feast of Freshness

- **Seafood Extravaganza:** Hokkaido is a seafood lover's paradise. The cold, pristine waters surrounding this northern island produce some of the best seafood in Japan. Think succulent crab, plump scallops, and the freshest sushi you've ever tasted. Sapporo's Nijo Market is a must-visit for seafood enthusiasts. Here, you can sample kaisen-don, a rice bowl topped with a variety of fresh seafood. Don't miss the chance to try Hokkaido's famous king crab, a true delicacy.

- **Dairy Delights:** Hokkaido is also known for its high-quality dairy products. The rich pastures of the region produce milk, cheese, and ice cream that are second to none. Head to Furano and Biei, where you can visit local farms and indulge in creamy soft-serve ice cream, buttery cheese, and fresh milk. Make sure to try the cheese tarts from LeTAO in Otaru – they are simply divine!

- **Top Dining Spots in Hokkaido:**

1. ***Sapporo Beer Garden:*** Enjoy fresh seafood and succulent lamb BBQ (jingisukan) paired with Sapporo beer.

2. ***Hakodate Morning Market:*** Feast on fresh seafood like squid and sea urchins in this bustling market.

3. ***Kaisen-Shokudo Kitano Gourmet-tei (Otaru):*** Delight in kaizen-don bowls brimming with fresh fish.

→ Hiroshima: Savory and Satisfying

- **Okonomiyaki Heaven:** Hiroshima's signature dish, okonomiyaki, is a savory pancake filled with a variety of ingredients like cabbage, pork, and noodles, then topped with a special sauce, mayonnaise, and bonito flakes. Unlike the Osaka version, Hiroshima-style okonomiyaki is layered, not mixed. For the best experience, head to Okonomimura, a building dedicated to okonomiyaki with numerous stalls serving their unique takes on this beloved dish.

- **Oysters Galore:** Hiroshima is also famous for its oysters, harvested from the Seto Inland Sea. These oysters are plump, juicy, and delicious whether grilled, fried, or served raw. Visit Miyajima Island for some of the best oyster restaurants, where you can enjoy this delicacy with a stunning view of the Itsukushima

Shrine.

- **Top Dining Spots in Hiroshima:**

1. ***Okonomimura:*** A multi-floor food paradise dedicated to Hiroshima-style okonomiyaki.

2. ***Miyajima Island:*** Try the grilled oysters and other seafood delights right on the island.

3. ***Hassei:*** A popular local spot in Hiroshima city known for its delicious and hearty okonomiyaki.

So, whether you're savoring the fresh seafood and dairy of Hokkaido or indulging in the hearty okonomiyaki and oysters of Hiroshima, these regions offer culinary experiences that are not to be missed. Pack your appetite and get ready for a gastronomic journey through some of Japan's most delicious destinations!

CHAPTER 9

Exploring Nagoya and Onsen: Uncovering Modern Marvels and Relaxation

Embrace the ninth tip by exploring the dynamic cityscape of Nagoya, followed by rejuvenating soaks in the serene onsen, for a perfect mix of excitement and relaxation.

The chapter "Exploring Nagoya and Onsen: Uncovering Modern Marvels and Relaxation" introduces you to the dynamic city of Nagoya and the traditional Japanese hot springs known as Onsen. You will learn about Nagoya's modern attractions and cultural landmarks, as well as the serene relaxation offered by onsen experiences.

9.1 Nagoya's Top Attractions

Ready to dive into the vibrant city of Nagoya?

Whether you're a history enthusiast, a car lover, or just eager to soak in some local culture, Nagoya is packed with amazing experiences. Let's explore some of the top attractions that should be on your list.

→ Nagoya Castle: A Historical Gem

Nagoya Castle is a symbol of the city's rich history. Originally built in 1612 by Tokugawa Ieyasu, the castle played a crucial role during the Edo period. It was partially destroyed during World War II but has since been reconstructed, including the majestic main keep adorned with golden shachihoko (mythical carp).

- **Historical Significance:** The castle was a strategic military base and a political center, reflecting the power and wealth of the Tokugawa shogunate. Inside, you'll find a museum showcasing samurai armor, historical artifacts, and detailed models of the original castle town.
- **Tips for Visiting:**

1. ***Best Time to Visit:*** Spring is ideal, as the castle grounds are covered with cherry blossoms.
2. ***Admission:*** ¥500 for adults, free for children under junior high school age.
3. ***Highlights:*** Don't miss Honmaru Palace with its exquisite sliding door paintings and traditional architecture.

→ Atsuta Shrine: A Spiritual Oasis

Atsuta Shrine is one of Japan's most significant Shinto shrines, dating back nearly 2,000 years. It houses the sacred Kusanagi-no-Tsurugi, one of the Imperial Regalia of Japan. This serene spot is perfect for those seeking a spiritual experience amidst lush greenery.

- **Cultural Significance:** The Atsuta Shrine is dedicated to Atsuta-no-Okami and five other deities. It's a popular site for traditional Japanese weddings and various festivals, including the Atsuta Festival in June.

- **Tips for Visiting:**

1. ***Best Time to Visit:*** Early morning for a tranquil experience and to avoid crowds.

2. ***Admission:*** Free.

3. ***Highlights:*** Explore the Treasure Hall, which exhibits over 4,000 relics, including ancient swords and mirrors.

→ Toyota Commemorative Museum of Industry and Technology: Innovation at its Best

For those fascinated by technology and automotive history, the Toyota Commemorative Museum of Industry and Technology is a must-visit. Located in the birthplace of Toyota, this museum showcases the evolution of Japan's leading automobile manufacturer from its origins as a textile company.

- **Historical and Cultural Significance:** The museum highlights Toyota's contributions to Japan's industrial development and technological advancements. It features interactive exhibits, demonstrations of historical weaving machines, and a comprehensive collection of cars, from the earliest models to the latest innovations.

- **Tips for Visiting:**

1. ***Best Time to Visit:*** Anytime, as the museum is indoors and climate-controlled.

2. ***Admission:*** ¥500 for adults, ¥300 for children.

3. ***Highlights:*** Don't miss the robotics and automobile sections, where you can see live demonstrations and even try your hand at some of the machines.

→ Extra Tips for an Enriching Visit:

- **Language Help**: While English signage is available, learning a few basic Japanese phrases can enhance your experience.
- **Travel Passes**: Consider getting a Nagoya Sightseeing Route Bus ticket for accessing easily to multiple attractions.
- **Local Cuisine**: Don't leave Nagoya without trying its famous hitsumabushi (grilled eel on rice) and miso katsu (pork cutlet with miso sauce).

From the storied walls of Nagoya Castle to the sacred grounds of Atsuta Shrine and the cutting-edge exhibits at the Toyota Museum, Nagoya offers a rich tapestry of experiences that blend history, spirituality, and modern innovation. Happy exploring!

9.2 Modern Landmarks in Nagoya

Are you ready to explore the cutting-edge side of Nagoya?

Hey there, fellow adventurers! This city isn't just about its rich history; it's also home to some incredible modern landmarks. Let's dive into the highlights of Nagoya's contemporary attractions and discover what makes them so special.

→ Nagoya TV Tower: A Sky-High Experience

First up, is the Nagoya TV Tower. Standing proudly at 180 meters, this architectural marvel offers breathtaking panoramic views of the city. Imagine yourself at the observation deck, soaking in the scenery. It's particularly stunning at night when the city lights sparkle like stars. Feeling thirsty? Head over to the Sky Deck Café—there's nothing like enjoying a refreshing drink while gazing over the urban landscape. Want a pro tip? Check the weather before you go for the clearest views!

→ Oasis 21: The Spaceship Aqua

Next on our list is Oasis 21, an architectural wonder that looks like it belongs in a sci-fi movie. Nicknamed the "Spaceship Aqua," this futuristic complex features a unique glass roof filled with water, creating a mesmerizing reflection of the sky. Underneath this amazing structure, you'll find a shopping and dining paradise with plenty of spots to relax. Make sure you don't miss the rooftop garden for some green space in the middle of the city. Here's an insider tip: Visit in the evening when the entire structure is beautifully illuminated—it's a sight you won't forget!

→ SCMAGLEV and Railway Park: A Train Enthusiast's Dream

For all your tech and train buffs out there, the SCMAGLEV and Railway Park is a must-visit. This museum is dedicated to the history and future of high-speed rail. Picture yourself getting up close with actual Shinkansen (bullet trains) and even the ground-breaking SCMAGLEV trains, which are set to revolutionize travel with their magnetic levitation technology. The interactive exhibits and simulators make it fun for all ages. Want a handy tip? Allocate at least half a day here to fully explore all the fascinating exhibits.

→ Exploring Tips :

- **Timing:** Plan your visit to the Nagoya TV Tower and Oasis 21 in the late afternoon to catch the sunset and see the city transition from day to night. It's a magical experience you won't want to miss.
- **Tickets:** Look out for combo tickets for multiple attractions—they often save money and time. It's a great way to maximize your adventure.
- **Transport:** Use the Nagoya City Subway for convenient and quick access to these landmarks. The Meijo Line and Higashiyama Line are particularly useful.
- **Apps:** Download a translation app to help with any language barriers, especially

for detailed exhibits at the SCMAGLEV and Railway Park. It makes navigating and understanding much easier.

By integrating these modern landmarks into your Nagoya itinerary, you'll experience the perfect blend of tradition and innovation. Get ready to be amazed by what this vibrant city has to offer! Have an awesome time exploring!

9.3 Introduction to Onsen: Japan's Traditional Hot Springs

Hello, relaxation seekers! If you're planning a trip to Japan, experiencing an onsen, or traditional hot spring, is an absolute must. Let's dive into the soothing world of onsen, exploring its cultural significance, types of experiences, proper etiquette, and some top destinations to visit for a truly relaxing and authentic Japanese experience.

→ Cultural Significance of Onsen:

Onsens are more than just a place to bathe; they're deeply embedded in Japanese culture and tradition. Historically, onsen were believed to have healing properties due to their rich mineral content. People would travel long distances to soak in these natural hot springs, seeking relief from ailments and stress. Today, onsen remains a cherished part of Japanese life, offering a perfect way to unwind and rejuvenate.

→ Types of Onsen Experiences:

Japan offers a variety of onsen experiences, each unique and delightful in its way:

- **Outdoor Onsen (Rotenburo):** Imagine soaking in a hot spring surrounded by breathtaking natural scenery. These outdoor baths offer a serene connection with nature, whether it's nestled in the mountains or overlooking the sea.
- **Indoor Onsen:** These baths are located inside traditional ryokans (Japanese inns) or modern hotels. They provide a controlled environment and are perfect

for those who prefer privacy.

- **Foot Baths (Ashiyu):** If you're short on time or just want a quick soak, try an ashiyu. These are shallow pools where you can dip your feet, often found in public areas and parks.
- **Public Onsen:** These communal baths are found throughout Japan and offer a social bathing experience. They're perfect for mingling with locals and experiencing the communal aspect of onsen culture.

→ Onsen Etiquette:

To fully enjoy your onsen experience, it's important to follow some basic etiquette:

- **Wash Before You Soak:** Always wash and rinse your body thoroughly before entering the onsen. Most facilities have shower areas for this purpose.
- **No Swimsuits:** Onsens are traditionally enjoyed without clothing. Some onsens provide a small towel for modesty, but it should not be taken into the water.
- **Keep Your Towel Out of the Water:** If you have a small towel, leave it on the edge of the bath or place it on your head.
- **Respect Silence:** Onsens are places of relaxation, so keep noise to a minimum to respect the tranquility of others.
- **Tattoos:** Be aware that some onsen may have restrictions on tattoos due to cultural reasons. It's best to check in advance or find a tattoo-friendly onsen.

9.4 Famous Onsen Destinations

Here are some top onsen destinations to consider:

- **Hakone:** Just a short trip from Tokyo, Hakone is famous for its picturesque onsen with views of Mount Fuji. It's a perfect getaway from the city.

- **Beppu:** Located on Kyushu Island, Beppu is known for its unique "Hells" hot springs and a wide variety of onsen experiences, from sand baths to mud baths.
- **Noboribetsu:** In Hokkaido, Noboribetsu boasts some of Japan's most nutrient-rich waters, with various baths to choose from, set in a stunning volcanic landscape.
- **Kusatsu:** This onsen town in Gunma Prefecture is renowned for its high-quality, acidic waters that are said to have exceptional healing properties.
- **Kinosaki:** A charming town in Hyogo Prefecture where you can enjoy a traditional onsen-hopping experience, moving from one bathhouse to another.

By immersing yourself in an onsen, you'll not only relax your body but also gain a deeper appreciation for Japanese culture and traditions. Enjoy your soak, and let the hot springs melt away your stresses and worries!

→ General Tips for Onsen Visits:

- **Respect the Etiquette:** Always wash thoroughly before entering the onsen and avoid bringing towels into the water. Keep noise levels low to maintain a tranquil atmosphere.
- **Hydrate:** Make sure to drink plenty of water before and after your soak to stay hydrated.
- **Avoid Onsen with Open Wounds or Infections:** It's important to stay out of the onsen if you have any open wounds or infections to maintain hygiene for all guests.

Embarking on an onsen adventure in Japan is not just about relaxation; it's about immersing yourself in a cultural experience that has been cherished for centuries. Whether you choose the scenic beauty of Hakone, the diverse springs of Beppu, or the mineral-rich waters of Noboribetsu, you're in for a truly rejuvenating treat. Happy soaking!

CHAPTER 10

Indulging in Japanese Cuisine: A Culinary Journey Across Japan

In tip ten, discover the essence of Japanese cuisine, from sushi and ramen to kaiseki and street food, for an unforgettable culinary journey.

The chapter "Indulging in Japanese Cuisine: A Culinary Journey Across Japan" takes readers on a flavorful exploration of Japanese food. Readers will learn about the rich culinary traditions, regional specialties, and iconic dishes that make Japanese food renowned worldwide, gaining insights into the flavors, ingredients, and cultural significance of each culinary delight.

10.1 Regional Culinary Specialties Across Japan

Embark on a delectable gastronomic journey through Japan's diverse regions, each offering its unique flavors and culinary traditions. From the northern island of Hokkaido to the southern paradise of Okinawa, let's explore the regional culinary specialties waiting to be savored across Japan.

→ Hokkaido:

Fresh Seafood: Imagine yourself indulging in succulent crab, sweet scallops, and buttery uni (sea urchin), all freshly harvested from Hokkaido's pristine waters. Which seafood delicacy would you be most excited to try?

→ Tohoku:

Grilled Sendai Beef: Picture yourself savoring the rich flavors of Sendai beef, grilled to perfection and served with savory accompaniments. How does the thought of biting into a tender slice of Sendai beef make your mouth water?

→ Kanto (Tokyo and Surrounding Areas):

Sushi and Sashimi: Envision yourself exploring the bustling seafood markets of Tokyo, sampling a variety of sushi and sashimi made with the freshest catches of the day. Can you already taste the delicate flavors of nigiri sushi and the exquisite texture of sashimi melting on your tongue?

→ Chubu (Central Japan):

Hida Beef: Close your eyes and imagine the aroma of sizzling Hida beef, its marbled texture promising a culinary experience like no other. How would you enjoy your Hida beef - as a succulent steak or in a comforting sukiyaki hotpot?

→ Kansai (Osaka, Kyoto, and Surrounding Areas):

Okonomiyaki: Visualize yourself sitting at a traditional okonomiyaki restaurant in Osaka, watching the chef expertly grill a savory pancake filled with your favorite ingredients.

Are you drawn to the classic flavors of pork and cabbage or tempted by more adventurous fillings?

→ CHUGOKU (HIROSHIMA AND SURROUNDING AREAS):

Hiroshima-style Okonomiyaki: Picture yourself in Hiroshima, indulging in the city's signature Okonomiyaki layered with noodles and grilled to perfection. Imagine the delicious interplay of flavors and textures in each bite.

→ SHIKOKU:

Sanuki Udon: Envision yourself slurping a piping hot bowl of Sanuki udon, its firm texture and rich flavor warming you from the inside out. Enjoy your Sanuki udon - with a simple broth or topped with a flavorful assortment of condiments.

→ KYUSHU:

Hakata Ramen: Imagine yourself sitting down to a steaming bowl of Hakata ramen, the rich aroma of pork bone broth tantalizing your senses. Customize your ramen with extra toppings and spice levels.

→ OKINAWA:

Okinawan Soba: Close your eyes and imagine the comforting aroma of Okinawan soba, its savory broth and chewy noodles warming your soul. Can you envision yourself savoring this beloved island dish on a beautiful Okinawan beach?

With its rich culinary heritage and diverse regional specialties, Japan invites you on a flavorful journey. From the snow-capped mountains of Hokkaido to the tropical shores of Okinawa, each region offers a unique culinary experience waiting to be discovered. So, pack your appetite and prepare for a gastronomic adventure through the vibrant flavors of Japan!

10.2 Seasonal Ingredients in Japan

Exploring Japan's culinary landscape is a year-round adventure, thanks to its emphasis on seasonal ingredients. Each season brings its unique produce, offering flavors that reflect the changing environment. Here's an informative guide to Japan's best seasonal ingredients and the delicious dishes that celebrate these fresh flavors.

SPRING: CHERRY BLOSSOMS AND BAMBOO SHOOTS

→ CHERRY BLOSSOMS (SAKURA):

Best Time to Enjoy: Late March to early April

- **Culinary Traditions:** Cherry blossoms aren't just for viewing but are also used in various culinary delights. Sakura mochi, a pink rice cake wrapped in a salted cherry blossom leaf, and sakura tea, made from preserved cherry blossoms, are popular spring treats.
- **Dishes to Try:** Sakura mochi, sakura tea, and sakura-flavored sweets and pastries.

→ BAMBOO SHOOTS (TAKENOKO):

Best Time to Enjoy: April to May

- **Culinary Traditions:** Bamboo shoots symbolize spring and are often enjoyed fresh. They're typically boiled or simmered to highlight their delicate flavor.
- **Dishes to Try:** Takenoko Gohan (rice cooked with bamboo shoots), miso soup with bamboo shoots, and tempura.

Summer: Japanese Plums and Ayu Fish

→ Japanese Plums (Ume):

Best Time to Enjoy: June

- **Culinary Traditions:** Ume is used to make umeboshi (pickled plums) and ume syrup. These plums are cherished for their tart and refreshing taste.
- **Dishes to Try:** Umeboshi, ume syrup drinks, and ume-flavored sweets.

→ Ayu(Sweetfish):

Best Time to Enjoy: July to September

- **Culinary Traditions:** Ayu are often grilled with salt and enjoyed as a seasonal delicacy. Their sweet, delicate flesh is a summertime favorite.
- **Dishes to Try:** Grilled ayu, ayu sashimi, and ayu rice.

Autumn: Matsutake Mushrooms and Kabocha Squash

→ Matsutake Mushrooms:

Best Time to Enjoy: September to November

- **Culinary Traditions:** Matsutake mushrooms are prized for their aromatic, earthy flavor. They are considered a luxury ingredient and are often featured in simple dishes to highlight their taste.

- **Dishes to Try:** Matsutake rice, Dobin mushi (steamed matsutake in a teapot), and matsutake soup.

→ Kabocha(Japanese Pumpkin):

Best Time to Enjoy: October to December

- **Culinary Traditions:** Kabocha is a versatile autumn ingredient used in both savory and sweet dishes. Its sweet nutty flavor and smooth texture make it a favorite in Japanese kitchens.
- **Dishes to Try:** Kabocha tempura, kabocha soup, and kabocha salad.

Winter: Yuzu and Daikon Radish

→Yuzu:

Best Time to Enjoy: November to January

- **Culinary Traditions:** Yuzu is a fragrant citrus fruit that is used to add a refreshing zest to dishes. Its juice, zest, and peel are used in various culinary applications.
- **Dishes to Try:** Yuzu miso, yuzu kosho (spicy yuzu paste), yuzu-flavored desserts, and yuzu hot pot.

→ Daikon Radish:

Best Time to Enjoy: November to February

- **Culinary Traditions:** Daikon is a staple winter vegetable in Japan, known for its crisp texture and mild flavor. It's often used in stews, pickles, and salads.

- **Dishes to Try:** Oden (a winter stew featuring daikon), grated daikon served with grilled fish, and daikon pickles.

Japan's seasonal ingredients offer a delicious and immersive way to experience the country's rich culinary heritage. Each season provides a unique opportunity to savor fresh produce at its peak, from the delicate sweetness of cherry blossoms in spring to the aromatic warmth of yuzu in winter. By enjoying these seasonal delicacies, you can truly taste the essence of Japan throughout the year. So, which season's flavors are you most excited to explore on your next visit to Japan?

10.3 Dining Etiquette and Customs in Japan

Dining in Japan is not just about enjoying delicious food but also about observing proper etiquette and customs. Here's a detailed guide to help you navigate the dining experience respectfully and enjoyably.

→ Proper Chopstick Use:

- **Holding Chopsticks:** Hold your chopsticks towards their end, not in the middle or front third. Use your dominant hand to manipulate them.

- **Avoid Pointing:** Never point your chopsticks at people or objects. It's considered rude.

- **Passing Food:** Do not pass food directly from your chopsticks to someone else's. This practice is reminiscent of a funeral ritual.

- **Sticking Chopsticks:** Never stick chopsticks upright into a bowl of rice. This resembles a practice associated with funerals and is considered very disrespectful.

- **Resting Chopsticks:** When you're not using your chopsticks, rest them on the provided chopstick rest (hashioki) or lay them horizontally on your plate.

→ Expressions of Gratitude:

- **Before Eating:** Say "Itadakimasu" (□□□□□□)□ which means "I humbly receive." It's a way of expressing gratitude for the food.
- **After Eating:** Say "Gochisousama deshita" (□□□□□□□□□), meaning "Thank you for the meal." This shows appreciation for the effort put into preparing the food.

→ Cultural Norms:

- **Slurping Noodles:** It's perfectly acceptable to slurp your noodles in Japan. It's considered a sign that you're enjoying your meal.
- **Eating Sushi:** When eating sushi, you can use your hands or chopsticks. Dip the fish side, not the rice side, into soy sauce to prevent the rice from falling apart.
- **Sharing Dishes:** Use the opposite end of your chopsticks to take food from shared dishes, not the end you eat from.
- **Drinking:** When drinking alcohol, it's customary to pour for others rather than for yourself. Hold your glass up to receive a pour and reciprocate by pouring for others.
- **Making Noise:** Avoid making loud noises while eating, except for slurping noodles. This includes talking loudly or chewing noisily.

→ Seating and Serving:

- **Seating:** Wait to be seated by the host. In traditional settings, you might be seated on tatami mats and low tables.
- **Serving Order:** In formal settings, wait for the eldest or highest-ranking person to start eating first.

- **Bowls and Plates:** Hold small bowls close to your mouth when eating from them, especially rice and soup. It's considered good manners.

→ Handling Money and Tips:

- **Paying the Bill:** When paying the bill, place the money on the tray provided rather than handing it directly to the cashier.
- **Tipping:** Tipping is not customary in Japan and can even be considered rude. Excellent service is expected without the need for additional gratuity.

→ Additional Tips:

- **Removing Shoes:** In some traditional restaurants, you might be asked to remove your shoes before entering. Always wear clean socks.
- **Use of Oshibori:** You'll be given a hot or cold towel (oshibori) to clean your hands before eating. Use it for your hands, not your face or neck.
- **Finishing Your Food:** It's polite to finish everything on your plate as it shows appreciation for the meal.

Dining in Japan is an experience rich in cultural traditions and etiquette. By following these guidelines, you can ensure that you dine respectfully and enjoyably. Whether you're savoring ramen, enjoying sushi, or experiencing a traditional kaiseki meal, these tips will help you navigate the dining customs with confidence and grace. So, are you ready to enjoy your Japanese dining adventure? Remember, it's all about respect, gratitude, and savoring each bite!

CHAPTER 11

Essentials and Maps: Must-Have Items and Navigational Resources

Last, but not least, In our final and concluding tip, we focus on the essentials and maps that will guide your journey, making your Japanese adventure seamless and enjoyable.

The chapter "Packing Essentials and Maps: Must-Have Items and Navigational Resources" provides you with practical guidance on what to pack for the trip to Japan and how to navigate effectively once you arrive. You will learn about essential items to bring, such as clothing, toiletries, and travel documents, as well as how to use maps and other resources to explore Japan's attractions with confidence.

11.1 Essential Packing List for Traveling to Japan

Let's make sure you have everything you need for an unforgettable adventure! Here's your comprehensive packing list to help you get ready:

→ Clothing:

- **Seasonal Clothes:** Packing the right clothes can make or break your trip, so let's get this right!

1. ***Spring (March-May):*** Expect unpredictable weather. Think light jackets, long-sleeve shirts, and jeans. Layers are your best friend here.

2. ***Summer (June-August):*** It gets hot and humid. Go for lightweight, breathable clothing like t-shirts, shorts, and summer dresses. A hat and sunglasses are essential to beat the heat.

3. ***Autumn (September-November):*** Similar to spring. Pack sweaters and scarves for those cool evenings. You'll want to enjoy the beautiful fall foliage comfortably.

4. ***Winter (December-February):*** Warm coats, sweaters, thermal layers, and gloves are a must. If you're heading to snowy regions, don't forget your winter boots.

- **Comfortable Shoes:** Trust me, you'll be walking a lot! Your best walking shoes are a must. Planning some hikes? Don't forget those hiking boots.

- **Socks:** Clean, hole-free socks are crucial, especially since you might be removing your shoes often.

→ Travel Documents:

- **Passport and Visa:** Ensure your passport is valid for at least six months beyond your stay. Check if you need a visa and have it sorted before you leave.

- **Travel Insurance:** Print out your policy details and keep a digital copy on your phone.

- **Itinerary and Accommodation Details:** Have printouts of your bookings and a digital copy for easy access.

→ Electronic Devices:

- **Phone and Charger:** Don't forget an international adapter! Japan uses Type A and B plugs.
- **Camera:** Capture all those beautiful memories. Bring extra batteries and memory cards.
- **Portable Battery Pack:** Keep your devices charged on the go.
- **Laptop/Tablet:** If you need it, bring it along with the charger.

→ Toiletries:

- **Toothbrush and Toothpaste:** While you can buy these in Japan, it's nice to have your preferred brands.
- **Shampoo and Conditioner:** Travel-sized bottles are convenient.
- **Deodorant and Personal Hygiene Products:** Again, familiar brands might be preferable.
- **Prescription Medications:** Bring enough for your trip, along with a copy of the prescription.

Specific Items:

- **Reusable Water Bottle:** Staying hydrated is key, especially if you're exploring all day.

- **Umbrella:** A compact one is useful for sudden rain showers.
- **Backpack or Daypack:** Perfect for carrying your essentials while sightseeing.
- **Hand Sanitizer and Wet Wipes:** Keep clean and germ-free, especially in public places.
- **Travel Guidebook or Apps:** Helpful for on-the-go information and tips.

So, ready to pack? Double-check this list to ensure you have everything you need for a smooth, comfortable, and enjoyable trip to Japan. Safe travels and have an amazing adventure!

11.2 Travel Gear and Accessories for Your Trip to Japan

Ensure you have the right travel gear and accessories that can make your journey smooth and enjoyable. Let's dive into the essentials you'll want to pack:

→ Portable Wi-Fi Devices:

- ***Why You Need It:*** Staying connected in Japan is crucial for navigating, translating, and staying in touch. Portable Wi-Fi devices provide reliable internet access wherever you go.
- ***Where to Get It:*** Rent one at the airport, pre-order online for pickup upon arrival, or book through your accommodation.

→ Power Adapters:

- **Plug Types:** Japan uses Type A and B plugs. Make sure your devices are compatible.
- **Voltage:** Japan operates on 100V. Check your electronic devices to ensure they can handle this voltage or bring a voltage converter.

→ Travel Pillows:

Comfort on the Go: Whether it's a long-haul flight or a train journey, a travel pillow can make a world of difference in comfort. Opt for a neck pillow that provides good support and is easy to carry.

→ Luggage Recommendations:

- **Size and Type:** Choose lightweight, durable luggage that's easy to maneuver. A medium-sized suitcase is usually sufficient for most trips.
- **Carry-On Essentials:** A backpack or a small carry-on bag for daily excursions is essential. It should be comfortable, with enough room for your essentials like water, snacks, a camera, and a guidebook.

→ Packing Cubes:

Organization: Keep your belongings neat and easily accessible. Packing cubes help organize your clothes and accessories, making packing and unpacking a breeze.

→ Portable Chargers:

Stay Powered: Keep your devices charged on the go. A high-capacity portable charger is a must, especially if you're out exploring all day.

→ Reusable Shopping Bags:

Eco-Friendly: Japan has a strong focus on reducing plastic waste. Carrying a reusable shopping bag is not only environmentally friendly but also handy for impromptu shopping.

→ Umbrella or Raincoat:

Weather Preparedness: Japan's weather can be unpredictable. A compact umbrella or a lightweight raincoat will keep you dry during unexpected showers.

→ Money Belt or Anti-Theft Bag:

Safety: While Japan is known for its safety, it's always a good idea to keep your valuables secure. An anti-theft bag or a money belt can help protect your belongings.

→ Reusable Water Bottle:

Hydration: Tap water in Japan is safe to drink, so carrying a reusable water bottle helps you stay hydrated and reduces plastic waste.

→ Noise-Canceling Headphones:

Peace: Perfect for flights, train rides, or even a bit of quiet time in a bustling city.

→ Language Translation Apps:

Communication: Download translation apps to help bridge the language gap. Google Translate is a popular choice.

→ Compact First Aid Kit:

Be Prepared: Pack a small first aid kit with band-aids, antiseptic wipes, pain relievers, and any personal medications.

By packing these must-have travel gear and accessories, you'll be well-prepared for a convenient and comfortable journey through Japan. Enjoy your travels, stay connected, and explore with ease!

11.3 Navigational Tools and Apps for Traveling in Japan

Equip yourself with the right navigational tools and apps to make your trip seamless and stress-free. Here's a detailed guide on essential apps you'll need for mapping, translation, public transportation, and local information.

→ MAPPING APPS:

Google Maps:

Why It's Essential: Google Maps is a versatile tool for navigating Japan's streets, finding attractions, and locating restaurants.

Features: Turn-by-turn directions, real-time traffic updates, public transportation routes, and reviews of places.

Tips: Download offline maps of areas you plan to explore to save data and avoid connectivity issues.

Maps.me:

Why It's Useful: Offers detailed offline maps which are perfect for travelers without constant internet access.

Features: Offline maps, turn-by-turn directions, and a comprehensive list of points of interest.

→ TRANSLATION APPS:

Google Translate:

Why You Need It: Helps bridge the language barrier by translating text, voice, and even images in real-time.

Features: Voice conversation mode, instant camera translation, handwriting translation, and offline translation packs.

Tips: Download the Japanese language pack for offline use.

Waygo:

Why It's Great: Specializes in translating Japanese text, especially useful for reading menus and signs.

Features: Instant translation using your phone's camera, no internet connection required.

PUBLIC TRANSPORTATION APPS:

Japan Travel by NAVITIME:

Why It's Essential: Provides comprehensive public transportation information, including train schedules, routes, and fare information.

Features: Offline search, route planning, and real-time train updates.

Tips: Use it to plan complex routes involving multiple transfers.

HyperDia:

Why You Need It: Offers detailed train schedules and routes, perfect for navigating Japan's extensive rail network.

Features: Route search, timetable, and fare calculation.

Tips: Check for the latest updates as HyperDia is continuously updated with new schedules.

Tokyo Subway Navigation for Tourists:

Why It's Useful: Specifically designed for tourists using Tokyo's subway system.

Features: Route planning, subway maps, and station information in multiple languages.

Tips: Use it for efficient navigation through Tokyo's complex subway network.

Local Information Apps:

Japan Official Travel App:

Why It's Handy: Provides official travel information, including emergency contact details, guides to sightseeing spots, and more.

Features: Offline access to travel guides, tourist information, and emergency contacts.

Tips: A great starting point for planning your daily itinerary.

Yelp:

Why You'll Love It: Useful for finding local restaurants, cafes, and attractions with user reviews and ratings.

Features: User reviews, photos, and ratings of local businesses.

Tips: Check out the reviews and ratings before choosing a place to eat or visit.

GuruNavi:

Why It's Essential for Foodies: A dedicated app for finding restaurants in Japan, with detailed menus and reviews.

Features: Restaurant search, menus, and user reviews.

Tips: Use the app to discover hidden culinary gems and make reservations.

Connectivity Tips:

Pocket Wi-Fi:

Why You Need It: Ensures you have constant internet access for using all these apps efficiently.

Where to Get It: Rent from the airport or order online for pickup.

By downloading and familiarizing yourself with these essential apps and tools, you'll navigate Japan's cities and countryside with ease, ensuring a stress-free and enjoyable adventure. Happy traveling!

11.4 Language Tools and Resources for Travelers in Japan

Heading to Japan but worried about the language barrier? Fear not! Here's a comprehensive resource guide on language tools and resources to help you communicate effectively and understand Japanese culture during your trip.

→ LANGUAGE APPS:

Duolingo:

Why It's Useful: Offers interactive language lessons for beginners, covering essential phrases and vocabulary.

Features: Bite-sized lessons, gamified learning experience, and progress tracking.

Rosetta Stone:

Why It's Great: Provides immersive language learning experiences through audio and visual exercises.

Features: Speech recognition, interactive lessons, and mobile app compatibility.

→ PHRASEBOOKS:

Lonely Planet Japanese Phrasebook:

Why You Need It: Contains practical phrases for everyday situations, including greetings, dining, and emergencies.

Features: Phonetic pronunciation guide, cultural insights, and useful tips for travelers.

Berlitz Japanese Phrase Book & Dictionary:

Why It's Handy: Offers essential phrases and expressions with easy-to-understand translations.

Features: Compact size, durable cover, and pronunciation guide for tricky words.

→ TRANSLATION DEVICES:

Pocketalk:

Why It's Essential: Enables real-time translation of conversations in multiple languages.

Features: Two-way translation, offline mode, and compatibility with various languages.

WT2 Plus Translator Earbuds:

Why You'll Love It: Provides instant translation between languages through earbuds.

Features: Hands-free operation, clear audio quality, and compatibility with smartphones.

→ Cultural Etiquette Guides:

Etiquette Guide to Japan: Know the Rules that Make the Difference!

Why It's Useful: Offers insights into Japanese customs, manners, and social norms.

Features: Practical tips for bowing, gift-giving, and dining etiquette.

Culture Smart! Japan: The Essential Guide to Customs & Culture

Why It's Great: Provides cultural insights and practical advice for navigating Japanese society.

Features: Understanding Japanese behavior, communication styles, and business etiquette.

→ Online Resources:

Japan Guide:

Why It's Handy: Offers comprehensive travel information, including cultural insights, travel tips, and destination guides.

Features: Detailed articles, travel forums, and user-generated content.

Japan National Tourism Organization (JNTO):

Why It's Essential: Provides official travel information, including event listings, transportation guides, and cultural highlights.

Features: Travel guides, maps, and practical tips for travelers.

→ Cultural Immersion Experiences:

Airbnb Experiences:

Why You Should Try It: Offers unique cultural experiences hosted by locals, such as tea ceremonies, cooking classes, and language exchange meetups.

Features: Authentic interactions, hands-on activities, and insights into Japanese culture.

By utilizing these language tools and resources, you'll enhance your travel experience in Japan, communicate effectively with locals, and gain a deeper understanding of Japanese culture. Embrace the journey and enjoy every moment of your adventure!

11.5 Mapping Out Your Itinerary: A Practical Guide to Planning Your Japan Adventure

Mapping out your itinerary for Japan is an exciting part of trip planning. Here's how to do it effectively:

→ Prioritize Destinations:

Start by listing the top attractions and experiences you want to include in your itinerary:

- **Must-See Landmarks:** Identify iconic sites like Tokyo's Shibuya Crossing, Kyoto's Fushimi Inari Shrine, or Osaka Castle.
- **Cultural Experiences:** Include activities such as tea ceremonies, and traditional festivals, or visit historical sites to immerse yourself in Japanese culture.
- **Hidden Gems:** Research off-the-beaten-path destinations or lesser-known neighborhoods for unique discoveries and authentic experiences.

→ Consider Travel Times:

Be mindful of travel distances and transportation options between destinations:

- **Travel Modes:** Research train schedules, bus routes, or domestic flights to determine the most efficient way to get from one place to another.
- **Time Allocation:** Allocate sufficient time for travel between locations, especially for longer distances, and factor in rest stops and meal breaks.
- **Avoid Peak Hours:** Plan activities during off-peak hours to minimize crowds and optimize your time.

→ Allow Flexibility:

While it's essential to have a structured plan, leave room for spontaneity and unexpected adventures:

- **Flexible Itinerary:** Build free time for unplanned activities, allowing you to explore local neighborhoods, stumble upon hidden gems, or relax and recharge.
- **Weather Contingency:** Have backup indoor activities or alternative plans in case of inclement weather, ensuring you can adapt to changing conditions.
- **Embrace Serendipity:** Be open to serendipitous encounters and local recommendations, which can lead to memorable experiences you hadn't anticipated.

→ Seek Local Insights:

Tap into local knowledge and resources to enrich your itinerary:

- **Local Recommendations:** Consult guidebooks, travel blogs, or online forums for insider tips and recommendations from residents and fellow travelers.

- **Cultural Events:** Check local event calendars for festivals, exhibitions, or seasonal celebrations that happen during your visit, adding depth and authenticity to your itinerary.
- **Stay Informed:** Keep abreast of any travel advisories, cultural customs, or safety tips relevant to your destinations to ensure a smooth and enjoyable journey.

By prioritizing destinations, considering travel times, allowing flexibility, and seeking local insights, you can create a well-rounded itinerary that captures the essence of Japan and ensures a memorable travel experience.

CHAPTER 12

Conclusion

In concluding our journey through the vibrant tapestry of Japan, I hope this guide has served as a faithful companion, illuminating the wonders and enriching experiences this captivating country has to offer. From the bustling streets of Tokyo to the serene landscapes of Hokkaido, from the ancient traditions of Kyoto to the resilient spirit of Hiroshima, we've traversed a diverse array of destinations, each with its unique charm and allure.

As we reflect on the memories we've made and the adventures we've shared, I encourage you to carry the spirit of exploration and curiosity with you beyond the pages of this book. Let the sights, sounds, and flavors linger in your heart, inspiring future travels and enriching your perspective on the world.

But our journey doesn't end here. As you embark on your Japanese adventure, I invite you to share your experiences with others. Whether it's through storytelling with friends and family or by leaving a review on Amazon, your voice has the power to inspire and guide fellow travelers on their explorations of Japan. Your feedback is invaluable, helping to shape future editions of this guide and ensuring that it continues to serve as a trusted resource for adventurers around the globe.

In closing, I sincerely thank you, the reader, for embarking on this journey with me. May the memories we've created continue to fuel your wanderlust and ignite your wonder. May your travels always be filled with discovery, joy, and endless possibilities.

Arigatou gozaimasu, and until we meet again on the roads less traveled.
Warmest regards,
V.Dharani Sudarvannan

Remember, your feedback is essential! If you found this guide helpful, please consider leaving a review on Amazon to share your experience with others. Your insights and recommendations are greatly appreciated and will help future travelers make the most of their adventures in Japan.

RESOURCES:

JNTO - Official Tourism Guide for Japan Travel (INDIA). (n.d.-b). Japan National Tourism Organization (JNTO). https://www.japan.travel/en/in

Tokyo. (n.d.-b). https://www.japan-guide.com/e/e2164.html

Nagoya. (n.d.). https://www.japan-guide.com/e/e2155.html

Osaka. (n.d.). https://www.japan-guide.com/e/e2157.html

www.ingramcontent.com/pod-product-compliance
Ingram Content Group UK Ltd.
Pitfield, Milton Keynes, MK11 3LW, UK
UKHW021408190726
13845UKWH00028B/962

9 789334 109566